# DANCING
## WITH GOD

A TRUE STORY

Marian Massie

Advanced Perceptions, Inc.
2010

The spiritual teachings mentioned in this text are those derived
from the author's personal experience and do not represent the official
positions of Eckankar. The intent of the author is only to offer information of a general nature to help you on your quest for spiritual, mental,
emotional, and physical growth. In the event you may use any of the
information in this book for yourself, which is your constitutional right,
the author and the publisher assume no responsibility for your actions.

Library of Congress Catalog Number Applied For

ISBN 978-0-9633140-0-0

Editor – Phyllis Mueller, Decatur, Ga.
Cover Design – Carol Renlie, Roswell, Ga.
Interior Design – Ellen Glass, Decatur, Ga.
Author's Photo – Brian Dougherty
Publisher – Advanced Perceptions, Inc., Roswell, Ga.

DEDICATION

## To Rajita (Judith)

*with Divine Love*

# Contents

# Ten Points or Rules for Being Human

ANONYMOUS

*You will receive a body.*

·

*You will learn lessons.*

·

*There are no mistakes, only lessons.*

·

*A lesson is repeated until learned.*

·

*Learning lessons does not end.*

·

*There is no better than here.*

·

*Others are merely mirrors of you.*

·

*What you make of your life is up to you.*

·

*Your answers lie inside you.*

·

*You will forget this.*

# Do I want to dance?

I WOKE UP IN A SWEAT, MY HEART ALMOST POUNDING
out of my chest. I frantically looked around my bedroom, afraid to remember my dream. Dreams had always
been my good friends, but this one disturbed me greatly.
I absolutely knew I would always remember this dream,
just like other powerful ones in my past, but this one left
an emotional baggage—fear. I understood I needed to confront it and learn what it meant, because if I didn't recognize what it was trying to convey it would continue to nag
at my peace of mind. This dream was a precognitive harbinger of things to come; just what it meant, I still needed
to sort out.

At the time of my dream, my husband and I lived in
a 1970s contemporary house that we were remodeling.
I was working at getting rid of the house's hunting-lodge-
on-steroids look, and converting it to a more modern style.

In this dream a woman with medium length, dark hair

came running up to me at that very house. I could only vaguely make out what she looked like. She was clearly panicked and came to me with fear in her voice, saying something was terribly wrong and desperately wanting my help.

Then the picture instantly changed. My viewpoint shifted, and I was looking at my house from outside. I saw water being drained from the house's plumbing. In a flash, the house slid off its foundation and was completely obliterated. Other houses around it were bathed in sunlight and calm. The woman had vanished, and I was left alone kneeling over the ruins of the house. All that was left now were new, green sprigs of trees sprouting where the house had been.

The next thing I remember was screaming in the dream at the top of my voice, "My life will never be the same again!" Real fear shot through me. Then I woke up. Terrified. I knew my life was going to change. A lot. My cursory understanding of this compelling dream was that something extremely hard was coming my way, and this dream was preparing me for the journey. Well, yippee . . . not!

CHAPTER

I

# The Power of Dreams

USUALLY I THINK OF NIGHTTIME DREAMS AS BEING very cool. They are the ultimate teachers, coming as they do from the deepest parts of our being. They can also provide much-needed emotional distance when you need this perspective for greater and more profound learning. When you're awake and analyze the dream or recount it, the depth of emotions you feel rarely equates to what you felt in the dream.

Dreams have a multitude of purposes. There are dreams that teach, dreams that help us process emotions, dreams of the future, and pure dreams that are real spiritual experiences. The true job of dreams is to help you understand yourself from a different perspective, so that you recognize mental or emotional habits you may want to break, deepen your connection to yourself as Soul, and open your awareness to the true Divine nature of life.

So why then did this dream still carry such emotional

weight with me? To answer that question I have to take you back to how I learned about the power of remembering dreams.

When I was about twenty, I had my first dream of the future. No one had to tell me what kind of dream it was; I just knew. (This is not always the case.) I was "dating" a married man at the time—something I don't recommend and I am not proud of. But as I look back on this choice, I have to admit it taught me many valuable spiritual lessons. One was that crossing a boundary and infringing on someone else will not uplift my life or anyone else's. This seems so utterly basic to me now, but at the time the word "boundary" was not even in my vocabulary.

In my first precognitive dream, I dreamt the wife of the man I was seeing was going to find the birthday card I had given him in the trunk of his car. This dream stuck with me; it was vivid, crystal clear and felt totally real. From having this dream, I knew this was how we would be found out, and that is exactly what happened! Having a dream that actually came true made me realize life was more inexplicable than it seemed. Part of me was very excited I had a new tool for learning that I recognized I could use in my everyday life. After that experience I looked forward to my dreams, started to remember more dreams, and gave them more reverence.

For weeks after I had the dramatic dream of the woman and my house sliding off its foundation, I would gently (and sometimes not so gently) focus on the meaning of it. I shared my dream with my good friends and asked their opinions. The real kicker here is that no one, not even close friends or people who write books, can tell you what your dreams mean, unless the interpretation presented really resonates with you.

Think about what you may have read to help you with understanding your dreams. Most of these books are filled with generalizations, and generalizations don't always apply. Just think about this for a moment: if I love cats, which I do, and you hate them, if we both dream of cats, the symbol of cats has to mean different things to each of us.

To understand your dreams you have to actively become aware of what the various things in the dream mean to you. No book or other person can take the place of your own internal investigation. Sometimes I am led, from my inner guidance, to look in a book for the meaning of something in a dream, but regardless of what the book tells me the dream means, I have to be the ultimate judge of its interpretation.

A fairly easy way to interpret what your dreams are telling you is to learn your own symbols. You do this by asking yourself questions. The most basic questions would be, "What does x mean to me and what does x symbolize or represent to me?"

Again, let's take my love of cats. Cats have always been in my life, giving me love and joy. When I see cats in my dreams I approach the dream with this in mind. This particular symbol is easy for me to recognize, so I gave the designation of love to cats. On the other hand, spiders scare me. Not as much as they used to, but it's safe to say I relate to spiders with more fear than inner peace and joy. So I have given spiders the designated symbol of fear and I interpret my dream with this in mind when spiders appear in my dreams.

When people you know in daily life appear in your dream, ask yourself the question: What does Sam or Mary represent to me? Never cop out and say, "I don't know." (As a professional clinical hypnotherapist/success coach, I never let my clients get away with saying, "I don't know" in their sessions.) When you do that you shut down your intuition and self-knowledge. This is totally counter-productive to what you want to accomplish through your dreams.

When you commit to knowing what your dreams are trying to communicate to you, the answers come, just like they do with my clients when they are in session with me.

**How to Remember Your Dreams**

Here is an easy method to remember your dreams.

Keep a pad of paper or a journal by your bed and write down everything you can remember when you first wake up.

Record everything, even small parts of dreams or just feelings you experienced in your sleep.

This practice will strengthen your memory of your dreams. Recalling dreams is like exercising a muscle. You have to use it to make it stronger. Focusing on dreams and writing them down in the morning when you wake is the way you strengthen your dream-muscle.

If you continue to be stuck, ask this question: "If I did know what *x* symbolizes, what would it be?" By phrasing the question this way, you open to your intuition through an inferential doorway of learning. Listen to what surfaces in your thoughts when you ask yourself that question. The answer will surface. No matter how silly or how illogical the answer may seem to you, give yourself time to digest it and assimilate the perspective it is trying to provide you. You will see your dreams and intuition tap the element of yourself that is different from the logical, intellectual part of yourself.

Understand dreams are trying to stretch your awareness in multiple dimensions. They can give you answers and directions for dealing with daily problems and help you grow as a person, in ways that may have eluded you intellectually. It is absolutely safe to remember your dreams and know what they mean. They are your friends. (Even the intense ones like mine.) They are presented to your consciousness to help you learn, get over bad habits, teach a lesson, or prepare you for the future, and some are very pure spiritual experiences. You can live your life with a quality and richness that you couldn't possibly have without remembering your dreams and working with them for the betterment of your life.

Since I have made a study of my own dreams and I am familiar with my symbols, my house has, in the past, represented my marriages. I had two previous dreams that were also precognitive in nature that dealt with the symbol of my house. The initial one I had was in my first marriage.

🐾 *Yes, I have been married more than once. Actually three times, and I am in a wonderful marriage now. To find out how I got there, you can read more about it in my first book,* You Are Soul.

*One thing I tell my clients is that I have gone through just about everything they have and have learned and grown from my experiences, and because I have gone through so much, it has helped me be a better therapist. But I digress.*

Toward the end of my first marriage, I had an incredibly vivid dream in which my house flattened in seconds. (Picture those buildings being blown up on TV, where they cave in and all the dust swirls around and the building is instantly gone—well, that is what my house being razed looked like in the dream.) I remembered the dream and wondered at the time if it was warning me of impending divorce. About a month or two after that dream, my first husband and I had separated and were filing for divorce. I filed this experience away.

About two years later, I remarried. It was rocky right from the beginning. About a year into the marriage, I had another dream of my house collapsing. My husband was gone, but in the dream I was left with insurance. The insurance to me was a symbol that I would be okay through this life process.

I truly loved my second husband, and since we were just into the start of the marriage, I really didn't want to think of divorce. I talked to a good friend and told her about my disquieting dream. I recounted that I was warned about my impending divorce from my first husband through a similar dream. She told me that I was probably just reading too much into this dream.

Remember me telling you to be your own judge of the meaning of any dream? Well, this is a case-in-point. At my core, I knew I was being prepared for yet another divorce. Shortly after this dream, we did, indeed, get a divorce.

Since I had two other marriages that ended in divorce, I was familiar with the signs that a marriage is winding down. This was (and is not) the case with my present husband. But when I had another dream about my house collapsing, of course I came to the conclusion that something out of my control was going to end my marriage, because my house, not a generic house, slid off its foundation in the dream. So you see, when I had the dream of my house sliding off its foundation, but knew my marriage was solid, I was scared that something very bad was going to happen to my husband because in the dream I was left standing over the new growth and he was nowhere to be seen.

For weeks I grappled with this fear and eventually came to an inner peace. If I were going to go through the experience of divorce or death, I couldn't control it anyway. I realized I would get through it because the dream showed me I would. But after awhile that explanation just did not register with me at my core. Finally, I just intuited that I was going to go through something big and difficult and I would learn from it, and that old beliefs from my past would be wiped away. Because my house was a 70s house, it being older signified previous beliefs and the fresh growth rising from the destruction symbolized new learning for me.

For a period of several weeks or months, this harbinger of "ick" was floating through my consciousness. I remember telling my very corporate husband that I was going to have to confront something soon that would be very dire. Being the supportive person he is, he smiled at me with an oh-come-on look and went back to whatever he was doing.

The meaning of the dream finally surfaced. And what I would have to face would be intense and difficult and test me to the very depth of my core.

CHAPTER

2

# A Telephone Call
## That Changed My Life

I N THE SPRING OF 2005 I WAS WORKING AT MY OFFICE, just cleaning up paperwork, when my phone rang. It was my older sister, Judith. We chatted about nothing in particular for a short time and then she quietly laid a big emotional bomb on me: Judith had found a lump under her arm. She didn't have a diagnosis yet, but she wanted me to know.

I was totally shocked. Judith had had breast cancer twenty-four years earlier. Coincidentally, several months earlier I was bragging to my friend Beth that my sister had truly won the war against cancer because it had been so many years since her cancer and she had been free of any recurrence. Wrong. I tried to stay calm as I talked to Judith. Inside I was crushed, but I still held out hope that the lump would be benign.

At home that evening I told my husband that this was probably what my frightening dream was preparing me for.

Life doesn't get too much harder than dealing with cancer, though I was still hoping against hope that Judith's cancer had not returned.

A week or two went by and Judith called me again. My worst fears came true. The cancer had come back. Stage four. There is no stage five. It was in her bones, but no major organs. I was devastated! I called another sister, Jean, and told her the crushing news. We both started to cry. Cancer had hit our family . . . again.

This kind of news would be hard for any family, but our family has dealt with cancer up-close and personal many times. My father died of cancer, as did my brother and my mother. This was déjà vu. My mom first had breast cancer when I was only five years old, and she eventually died from it when the cancer metastasized to her bones when I was twenty-one. Twice in the same family, repeating the exact, same pattern. What were the odds?

## CHILDHOOD HISTORY

This news hit me especially hard, as my sister Judith was like my surrogate mom when I was a kid. Thirteen years older, she took care of me when my mom was too sick. I don't have conscious memories of this, but there had always been a special bond between Judith and me, even though we had very different personalities.

Judith, from my perspective, was always extremely serious. She was an artist and an academic, less social and mainstream than I, incredibly smart and talented, and particularly good with details. I, on the other hand, am a person who loves to laugh, to fly by the seat of my pants; I'm more mainstream and social and I do my research from my intuition and dreams. My sister's work was, I think, her whole life. She was married for a few years in her twenties and never married again, and she had no children.

Though Judith's life was quite different from mine, I never thought her path was wrong or less-than. I believe we come into this Earth-existence to continue to evolve as Soul, to learn how to live from a consciousness of Divine Love. We all have karma—good and bad—and each lifetime is a particular school or field of study for each individual. The family we are born into and the people we encounter along our journey give us opportunities to learn, clear karma, and share.

We came from a big Catholic family. My mom and dad had eight kids. I was the youngest and Judith was the second eldest. Judith left our family home when she was eighteen to become a nun. She left right around the time my mom had her first bout with breast cancer.

Watching from an upstairs bedroom window as Judith

left for the nunnery, I was grief-stricken. She had been my second mom from the time I was born. At five years old, I had no words to comprehend what was happening. From that moment on, though, I felt a part of me shut down against people leaving, and I developed an aversion to being around sickness. I became extremely self-contained and self-sufficient.

Trying to digest the shocking news of the resurgence of Judith's cancer, I sat on our screened porch at home. Right there and then, and I made an internal commitment to be present for my sister through her whole journey this time. During her first bout with cancer I did not show up for her in any way, and Judith, for the most part, handled it all by herself, without the emotional support of her brothers or sisters. (This may seem very strange until you look deeper into the dynamics of our family.)

We were raised in the '60s with an extremely sick mother and none of the outside support systems that people can tap into today. Since my mom was diagnosed with breast cancer when I was five, I never knew her well or happy. She had major depression and anxiety, along with many other serious physical aliments, until she died, when I was twenty-one. Even though I was the youngest, I was given an extreme amount of responsibility. My mother came to rely on me almost exclusively to take care of the house, since all of the other kids were mostly grown and gone.

By the time I was ten, I kept the house and did the weekly grocery shopping and the daily cooking. Later, through my own therapy and inner healing I came to understand that my mom used me, albeit unconsciously, to nurture herself emotionally also. Memories are seared in my brain of my mom in constant pain. The operation for her breast cancer left her horribly scarred; she basically looked as if she had been butchered. Her suffering was extensive, and consequently she became addicted to Valium and alcohol. Many times I'd come home from school and she'd be incoherent. There was even a time I had to pick her up off the floor because she was so drugged that she couldn't stand up.

Even so, I believe she handled her illnesses the best way she could. My mother was basically a very good person with terrible coping skills. The emotional backlash of having a mom so incapacitated and a father who was never engaged in our lives because he worked all the time was that all the kids in our family fended for themselves. All my brothers and sisters are pretty strong and smart, with unique personalities. We all survived the best way we could. I was the youngest and I survived by not emotionally bonding to my family until later in life. I virtually had no nurturing or guidance like a normal child would be have. What felt safe for me was to retreat inward and try to make sense of my life and what was happening in my family.

All of us were faced with one extremely sick mom and we all thought she was at the brink of death constantly. We were shell-shocked from disease, had no parental support, and consequently experienced very little joy. One of my earliest memories of the effect of this kind of exposure to prolonged sickness had on me is from kindergarten, when an unfamiliar adult came into the classroom. I immediately thought the stranger had come to tell me my mom had died. That fear was always in the background of my thoughts and feelings, as I am sure it must have been for the rest of my brothers and sisters.

Judith's first bout with cancer came a few years after my mom died. By then I was so numb from almost twenty years of dealing with my mom's tragedy that I had nothing left to give. I don't think at that time that I even knew how to give or allowed myself to have the luxury of feelings. I was grappling with learning how to get out of basic survival mode to some semblance of normalcy. I just could not handle another family member having cancer—and breast cancer, at that.

At the time, I was getting married for the first time

(a whole other story), and my fiancé was in chiropractic school. Judith lived in California and I lived in Atlanta, and during that time period we saw each other infrequently. Regardless, I intensely regret not even talking to her about her treatment and what she must have been going through emotionally. That is why I made my firm commitment to not run away from helping her go through this the second time. I knew it would be a long haul and be very difficult for Judith, as well as for me. Life had presented me a second chance to help my sister and heal old wounds of my own. Now I was in a much healthier place to be supportive, even though I knew how incredibly formidable it was going to be to confront this consciously instead of superficially.

After I inwardly made my promise, I sat down with my husband and told him what to expect: that supporting Judith emotionally would be daunting, probably long, and I was going to support her emotionally until the end of her journey.

This was totally new territory for me. I really did not know how to support someone with a life-threatening disease. Even though my father and mother and brother had died of cancer, I was not physically there to help them when they were dying nor did I check in emotionally with them to support them in any way. Supporting my sister—

to me—meant listening to her without telling her what
to do.

When I was around twenty-four I started a daily
practice of spiritual contemplations with the Light and
Sound of God. I found that the daily exercises of focusing
on the spiritual part of life helped me in every area of my
life. From this constant practice I felt like I was being fed
at the core of my being. Consequently, each year I was becoming happier and more confident.

Keeping up with my spiritual practice at this time
became invaluable, not only to nurture me throughout
this life cycle, but to help me heal what I needed, to be a
clear, strong support for my sister. And, quite frankly, I
wanted to face my own fear of death.

## SPIRITUAL EXERCISES

An extremely powerful spiritual exercise is repeating a
Spiritual Sound, a mantra, which is an actual vibration of
God or the Holy Spirit. There are many different highly
charged sounds or words—most people are somewhat
familiar with the word OM. The word I mainly use is HU.
Pronounced HUUUUUUUU, like the word hue. HU is
an ancient name for God. (In my book, *You Are Soul*, I
explain in more depth how to use different Spiritual

Sounds to elevate your daily life.)

Someone told me about using a mantra when I was in my mid-twenties. The idea interested me because it was more active than the meditation I was attempting. Spiritual exercises are different—more active—than the passive form of meditation. (When I tried meditation, clearing the mind, I would fall asleep. I knew that was not going to get me very far.) I was at the lowest point in my life at the time I learned about using Spiritual Sound as a way to uplift my consciousness.

Remember the dysfunctional childhood I told you about? Well, my childhood took a toll on me with an extensive eating disorder—bulimia; I would throw up about four or five times a day, sometimes as often as eight times a day. I became bulimic at fourteen and it lasted for thirteen years. No matter what I did, I could not stop. It was just as real an addiction as heroin to me, but no matter what I did nothing helped me stop this behavior. I realize now it was how I dealt with my emotions, through the cycle of eating and throwing up. When I look back at this period of my life, I probably was extremely depressed.

I had run away from home when I was fifteen and worked my way through school. Having had little or no guidance, my choices in relationships and other aspects of my life left a lot to be desired. Strangers would come up to me and ask me to smile, telling me I was the saddest person they had ever seen. (Well, thanks for sharing. Those comments surely lifted my spirits! Most of the time I just ignored those people, but in my mind I wanted to punch them. I'll show you sadness, all right!)

In my heart I knew those people were right, though. They could see the hole in my soul that nothing could fill, and the tremendous and overwhelming sorrow that did not go away until I worked with Spiritual Sound.

When I first started to work with Spiritual Sound on a daily basis I had been bulimic for thirteen years. I had given up all hope of conquering this debilitating problem. The unfathomable melancholy I mentioned earlier was ever present. It felt like I had a black hole in my heart that was impenetrable. I had absolutely no joy. I worked with Spiritual Sound just to see if I could even have any happiness or joy. When I would chant my mantra each day, I did not direct the Sound or the process with any intention to get rid of my bulimia. (By that time I had given up all hope of getting rid of it anyway.) I would sing or chant the Sound until I could feel a little lightness peeking through my heart. I did this diligently every day. To my astonishment, by the end of the third month my bulimia just went away! I had not visualized for it to be gone. I did not direct the Sound to clear it. Just singing it daily had changed me. As I started to sing this word daily, my profound sadness started to lift. I kept singing it every day, and every day I would feel a little bit better. It's like I connected to a power source of Divine Love.

My experience with having bulimia for thirteen years and then having it disappear when I worked with Spiritual Sound showed me once again that God communicates with us every day in different ways. The profundity of this experience will always live inside my heart. This was not an intellectual understanding of God or Spirit—it was an actual life-changing experience of the hand of God.

Think of Spiritual Sound as a true connection with the Holy Spirit. You do not have to change your religion or even have a religion to experience the power of any Spiritual Sound. It is part of Divine Love. God is Divine Love, and connecting more fully with Divine Love has to change your life for the better. We all exist because God loves each being!

Working with Spiritual Sound strengthens me from the inside out, not only when I was depressed, but now in my daily life. I came to rely on this inner strengthening to help me help my sister from a deep spiritual place, without trying to control her or cross her emotional, mental, or spiritual boundaries. The process of supporting Judith was very much like a dance. I would follow her lead, careful not to trespass on her growth, desires, and boundaries.

I knew things she did not, like my prophetic dream. Because of the dream, I always felt she would die from this disease. I never let Judith know about this particular dream. One reason I didn't is that I could have been wrong about the interpretation; even if I knew for certain, telling her or even hinting at this outcome would not only be cruel to Judith, but was also totally against the spiritual law of non-interference. I felt my job of supporting her during her journey was to listen, to be an objective sounding board. I did not tell her what doctor to go to or what treatment to have. I honored—to the best of my ability— her wishes. I believe my sister Jean did the same thing.

Though it may run counter to many people's beliefs, I never prayed or visualized for Judith's recovery. My spiritual practice taught me to ask for her highest good, not my desire for her healing or her wish to be healed. Really, no one knows what others need as Soul for their growth. That was true for my sister as well. Instead of praying for her healing, I sent her Divine Love. When she asked for my opinion, I would be honest but not attached to whether she did as I suggested. Inwardly, I always relinquished any attachment to an outcome, and I tried never to step on her authority. Each person is in charge of his or her ultimate growth as Soul. This is a huge lesson for most people:

getting out of the way of others.

Everyone has a unique path home to God. Your path can change in your lifetime, or you may need only one. I started out Catholic, tried atheism for a nanosecond, and was an agnostic, then Buddhist. What I practice now is Eckankar.

My strong convictions regarding working with Sound and Spirit are rooted in coming from a very dysfunctional family. I was always desperately lonely. Being the youngest, by the time I was nine or ten most of my siblings were gone from our house. I had way too much responsibility and no one to share my thoughts and feelings with, so I turned inward and developed a strong connection to Spirit-God. Though we were raised Catholic, that path never resonated with me. As a child, I went to church, but I felt something was missing for me. I was always consciously looking for my unique path.

I started hearing Spiritual Sound around the time I was eight or nine. When I went to bed I would hear this intense humming noise, like the sound of high-voltage wires. There were no high-voltage wires anywhere near our house—I always wondered what this sound was. As a child I was a little afraid, but inwardly I think I knew I was connecting to something greater than myself. Being a self-contained child, I never told anyone about this. My inward searching and connection helped me through my childhood, sometimes very dramatically.

Here is a perfect example of how connecting to Spirit helped my life in an incredibly dramatic way: It was when I was in elementary school and I was doing my homework at my little desk in my bedroom. My desk was situated against the wall near the door. I usually closed my door when I did my homework, and it was closed that night, so I was unaware of what my brother Robert was up to. Robert was home from the Marines, having been recently discharged.

I was minding my own business, being the good little student, when Robert got it into his head to clean his very big handgun in his bedroom, which was across the hall from my bedroom. Because he was a well-trained Marine, you would think he knew how to safely clean a gun. I did not know—nor did anyone know—he was cleaning his gun. In his great wisdom, he decided to point the gun inside the house, "just in case it went off, so [he] wouldn't break a window." Not the brightest idea to come down the pike, I think.

ᐸᑐ. *My brother Robert was always an accident waiting to happen: One time he ordered very volatile gunpowder by mail-order (try doing this nowadays!) and just by his sneezing too close to it, it exploded and singed off his eyebrows and eyelashes! You could never do this now, but this was in the '60s when life was more innocent and when your accident-prone brother could order gunpowder through the mail.*

I remember hearing a loud voice yell at me, "Move to the bed now!" The voice was commanding and clear, as if someone were yelling right next to me. I moved to my bed ... fast! Then I heard this deafening bang. It couldn't have been more than a split second after I moved from my desk chair and sat on my bed, that Robert's gun went off. I felt the bullet glance my hair, missing my head by millimeters. If I had stayed at my desk the bullet would have gone through my temple. The hole the bullet made in the wall was right where my head had been!

After the gun went off, my brother realized, "Oh, the bullet might have gone through the walls." Yah think? The bullet went through four walls and two pairs of my best shoes before it stopped. It was a BIG bullet! Robert then ran into my room, yelling my name. I was mute. I just didn't have it in me to say I was okay. Needless to say, he got into some big trouble with our parents!

As a child and young adult, I never revealed how that voice saved my life. No one had heard the voice except me. I remember it like it was yesterday. That voice was

Spirit helping me. That voice was part of the Spiritual Sound—God.

Spiritual Sounds come in different ways. Besides someone singing a Sound, like HU, Spiritual Sounds can be heard when you are not doing anything to create them, like the voice I heard that saved my life. You can hear inwardly or outwardly the sound of a single flute, thousands of violins, or the buzzing of bees. Water running, thunder, and electrical humming are also common Sounds. You may even hear your name being called out, when no one is there. That happened to me when I was at an extremely low point in my life when I was living on my own at sixteen. I heard my name called out and there were no people to be seen anywhere. I was starting to read more esoteric books at the time and I remember thinking, "Maybe a spiritual guide or angel was trying to connect with me." After that realization I didn't feel so alone.

When you hear these sounds it means Spirit, the Holy Spirit, is connecting with you to uplift your consciousness. You should never direct the Sound. You simply sing the HU or other highly charged words and let God or Spirit flow through you. This way you are being uplifted for your highest good and the good of others. Your will is never greater than God's. When I sing the HU, I open my heart and let the energy of HU flow through me.

Another significant time I heard the Sound out loud was when I went with my friends, Beth and Carol, to Charleston for a girls' weekend. We were in our mid-thirties and single. We were returning home to Atlanta after a nice weekend at the beach—three cute, blond women driving in a car, having fun, not a care in the world. We quickly caught the eye of this guy alone in his car and the three of us, all at once, felt we were in grave danger. There were no other cars on the highway at the time, and this was before cell phones. We felt extremely vulnerable and scared. The three of us knew about chanting or singing HU to grow spiritually, and worked with it often. So immediately we stared to sing HU out loud. We didn't know what else we could do for protection. By singing the HU at this time we were putting our safety into the hands of God. We did not direct the HU to stop the other car; we just sang this Spiritual Sound from the bottom of our hearts and kept on driving.

After half an hour, more cars appeared on the highway, and the car with the scary guy just disappeared. We all stopped chanting at the same time, feeling a great sense of relief and gratitude. Well, the sound of the HU continued without us singing for several minutes! We all heard the Sound and were blown away by the experience. (Since we all heard it, no one could say it was "only" our imaginations.)

Another very powerful time was when I was living with my best friend Beth in her house, between husband number one and husband number two. (That is another story for a different time.) Beth is a musician, and at that time she played many piano gigs at night. We operated on opposite schedules. I got up early to see clients during the day; she got up late and worked at night until about midnight or one in the morning. She was also writing music for her first CD at that time. Her studio was her computer and a synthesizer in her spare bedroom, which was across the hall from my bedroom.

I usually went to bed by ten-thirty. That night I was startled awake around midnight by really loud, but hauntingly beautiful, violin music. As divine as the music sounded, I was a bit peeved at Beth for working on her music so loudly in the middle of the night. It seemed totally out of character—Beth is extremely sensitive to other people. She is originally from North Dakota, where they surely must teach niceness, and she would never knowingly hurt anyone. I got up, as I said, quite irritated and ready to yell at her for being so insensitive. I dashed across the hall to the other bedroom and found no one there. Then the music just stopped. I called out to Beth. Beth was still at work. No one was home but me!

That time period for me was extremely hard: I was going through my first divorce and felt very raw and alone. I believe I heard the Sound to remind me that I am always loved and connected to God. I must have needed this extraordinary experience of the Holy Spirit uplifting my life at that time.

Please understand if you choose to work with Sound, your experiences will be different than mine. Each person—each Soul—has the experience that helps him or her grow, so no two people have the same experiences.

# Judith's Choices

JUDITH HAD BLOOD TESTS AND SCANS TO SEE WHAT course of action would be best for her. Since she was a very good detail-person and quite a researcher, Judith wanted to find the best team for her: a combination of an oncologist and holistic practitioners. She was also a spiritual seeker and aspired to live the higher spiritual laws to the best of her ability. This meant taking full responsibility for her actions, thoughts, and emotions.

Quality of life was paramount to Judith. Doing treatments that might extend her life but would take away the ability to think or have energy were not options for her.

She also lived with the belief that we are the sum of our choices—conscious and unconscious. Our real reason we are born into this life is to grow spiritually–which is, more simply, how to love–and we each have to deal with our positive and negative karma. Judith was aware of all of this. As she was finding what was right for her body, at the same time she was also working inwardly to change and evolve at a spiritual level.

I can only report the essence of what I experienced with her. I obviously don't know what her awareness and consciousness really were. She worked extremely hard on herself—that I do know.

## JUDITH'S PROFESSIONAL LIFE

Her profession was hard to categorize. After Judith left the nunnery in her twenties, she went on to get a Masters degree in Fine Art, and moved to Montana with her then-husband. At the time, she was a potter and he was a glass-blower. They helped run a foundation for the arts there for several years. I went to visit her there a couple of times before I ran away from home when I was fifteen.

Judith's art was always innovative. Most people at the time worked with heavy brown clay, very earthy, but she developed this beautiful style of pottery with white porcelain. Her glazes were a very sophisticated combination of purples, roses, and other colors, which I personally found much more beautiful. Judith always had more of an earthy, bohemian nature than me; I like makeup, to dress up and—good grief!—I like to golf.

Eventually she divorced her husband and moved to

the San Francisco Bay area, Sausalito, to be exact, where she lived in a small, but pleasant, rented apartment for about twenty years. Her place even had a view of the ocean.

During that time she made her living as a part-time art teacher at City College. I visited her there numerous times, and she seemed happy enough. During the time she was teaching, she stopped making pottery and started to do abstract oil paintings.

Her first paintings, in my opinion, were dark in nature, but very quickly she developed a style that reflected lightness in energy and color. She sold many paintings but always struggled financially. Judith made very little money and lived simply, in an almost austere way. I personally think that was a leftover energy from being a nun so many years ago.

As she grew spiritually, her art developed and the basis for most of her art then was the mandala. In Sanskrit, *mandala* means "circle." I Googled the meaning of *mandala* and this pretty well sums up the meaning of the word: "*A mandala is a symbol of integration and transformation. A tool for healing and bringing oneself into harmony to realize true self. Consists usually of a design within a circle symbolizing unity, the design mandala is a part of many cultures and can be created in various styles.*"

Since the circle is a symbol of perfection, eternity, unity, and completeness, Judith loved the idea and the form of the mandala. Her art pieces at that time conveyed beauty, balance and stunning color.

She went on to write a book about using color and art to tap into your spiritual self. The book was aptly titled *Mandala*. Judith, at the time, I think, was going through an immense spiritual growth. She put her emerging awareness into her art and into teaching others.

My sister and I were kindred spirits, although the ways we lived were quite different. Even though we knew the same spiritual talk ("spiro-speak" as my wonderfully irreverent husband calls it), walking that talk and living it are two different things. I was tested many times through her whole journey of cancer to walk my talk, to be kind and avoid pontificating. Even the best relationships are tested because of conflicting opinions, slights or invalidations, and family members can naturally push the biggest buttons you have. Through my inner commitment to face whatever I need to face within myself to be a clear channel of Divine Love and support for my sister, my unconscious issues surfaced with the natural course of our relating.

**Knowing and Healing**

Knowing higher spiritual teachings from an intellectual place is the first step in awareness. But you can have very different beliefs subconsciously and intellectually, and that disconnect will block your spiritual awareness and personal growth. The subconscious is ninety percent of your mind's power. You can tell if there is a disconnect between your intellect and subconscious if you know what to do and you are not doing it, or if you have been trying to change or achieve something for a long period of time and it is not manifesting. For example, if someone wanted to lose weight and knew all the appropriate foods to eat and how to exercise and just didn't do it, I would bet that person had different beliefs intellectually and subconsciously, or was not healthfully dealing with his or her emotions. Most people cannot—or will not—address healing subconscious emotions.

For example, I had a very wealthy client who came to me when she was in her mid-fifties. I will call her Grace. Grace desperately wanted to feel happy. She had always done exceedingly well in business, but happiness seemed to elude her. When she started sessions with me, I asked her to rate the quality of happiness she experienced most of the time. Rating herself from one to ten—ten being the happiest—she said she was around a one for most of her life.

Grace had tried every kind of therapy you can imagine. She took anti-depressants and went to expensive places for treatment, but still she did not experience the joyfulness in life she wanted. Intellectually, Grace could tell me exactly why she was this way, and she was absolutely correct in her assessment. But as I have said before, understanding something intellectually doesn't mean you have integrated the knowledge and healing into your subconscious or emotional self.

After working with me in therapy for about three months and changing her subconscious negative limiting beliefs and emotions, Grace started to feel happy! When I asked her again, on a scale of one to ten—ten being the happiest—where she was now, Grace said she felt like an eight. She literally started to cry, as this was the first time in her life she felt this good. In my therapy, I help clients change core subconscious beliefs and emotions that keep them from reaching their goals, not just understand their issues intellectually.

Spiritually we can have the same predicament. We can understand many of the higher principles of God and of life, but integrating them, living them, is what creates Spiritual growth.

## MY COMMITMENT TO JUDITH

My vow to support my sister emotionally during her journey encompassed the law of Divine Love. I put it out of my mind to teach, lecture, or make her feel wrong for her beliefs or choices. Even though it seemed we knew the same kind of teaching, we were on different spiritual paths. For me, my lesson was of being an emotional support and listening. Judith needed to talk and to have a trusted confidant. Many times, however, I perceived that Judith spoke to me as a teacher speaking to a student who didn't know anything, instead of someone having a conversation with a peer. During those times I would sing HU silently to myself, asking to relate from a loving and supportive place, instead of a place of power or ego. If I tried to tell her how to do something or what to do, she would not have felt

Spiritual
Principles in
Daily Life

What you do every day can shed the old clothes of a lesser way of being and contribute to revealing the higher nature of Divine Love within you. It is action, not intellect, which enables you to grow spiritually.

In the book *Stranger by the River,* Paul Twitchell sums up nicely what I want to convey. In the chapter about Love, Paul says, "Love is absolute. But the conception of love varies with the individual consciousness." He goes on to say, "Love is not a matter of belief. It is a matter of demonstration. Therefore, if you desire love, try to realize that the only way to get love is to give love. That the more you give the more you get; and the only way you can give is to fill yourself with it, until you become a magnet of love."

This is an ideal I strive for through my actions each day.

supported. Then I would have been coming from my ego, to be looked up to or to be validated, instead of being a vehicle of Divine Love. I really do not think she intended to preach, and more times than not, we had loving conversations. Providing a supportive ear was a way for me to put Divine Love into action with my sister. Walking my talk.

About two and a half years into her journey, Judith began in earnest using natural supplements geared toward healing cancer, as well as the drugs she could tolerate. The lump that was near the nerve in her arm started to shrink! Yippee!

At this juncture my sister Jean and I started using a tag-team approach with Judith. We found she would not tell one person all the things she was doing or experiencing. After one of us talked to Judith, we would call the other and compare notes. We did this for several years. We needed to do this since Judith lived in California and Jean and I were on the East Coast. Jean and I felt so helpless many times, but our communication with each other strengthened both of us to be able to help Judith, and gave each of us a real support system.

Judith's physical pain at this time was minimal, but my emotional pain regarding her cancer returning was starting to surface in incredibly strong ways. When I talked to Judith I kept my worry and concern out of my voice— or tried to, anyway. My self-talk through this whole thing was, "I want to be strong to support my sister." I didn't feel I could support Judith if I came across as an emotional basket case. So I hid my sorrow and grief from her. Being a therapist, I know emotions are energy. You cannot stuff them down without them popping up in some other way that eventually will hurt you. I did cry some, but the deep subconscious anchors regarding cancer, my mom—and now my sister—were really huge for me, and starting to affect me physically.

## FACING MY GRIEF

During this time, my husband Mark and I finished the second phase of remodeling our house. The old '70 s house was thankfully fading away, and a beautiful, new, elegant form was emerging. Part of this renovation was transforming our indoor, full-size racquetball court into a movie theater and library/ game room. Yes, you read right! Well, let me tell you, unless you really—and I mean *really*—like playing racquetball, a racquetball court in your house is like having a black hole that sucks the life, beauty, and utility out of your home. (Can you tell I hated it?) The size of it was daunting. It was two stories high and over two thousand square feet in size. So, what does one do with a windowless room that big? Our solution was to cut it horizontally and make the top half a movie theater and library/game room. We left the bottom half for storage.

One day while I was watching TV on the ten-foot screen in our new movie theater, the room literally started spinning–and, no, I was not drinking adult beverages at the time. I turned to my husband and calmly said, "I think I need some help handling my emotions about my sister." Then I proceeded to break down and sob. He took me in his arms and comforted me, but from this experience I knew I needed outside professional help.

We talked about my getting some help. Mark happened to personally know a therapist who specializes in dealing with grief. Well, that sounded perfect for me. Grief was surfacing faster than I could handle it. My husband is always supportive. When I need to cry he does all the right things, but I knew I needed more, and frankly it would not be good for our marriage if I used him as my therapist. Too often people rely on their spouses for all of their emotional support, to the detriment of their relationship. So I called the therapist that very day.

I had met her and her husband previously a couple of times. Mark knew her from his corporate days, and we saw them socially about every two years. Not exactly close friends, but I knew her well enough that I felt she would be a good starting point for my healing. I will call her Barb.

I met with Barb the next day. Barb has a warm "mom" kind of energy. Her specialty is assisting people who have gone through huge crises—like Hurricane Katrina victims —and she helps them deal with their tremendous loss and grief.

She saw me at her home-office. I spent most of an hour and half sobbing. It felt so good to cry!

Barb and I are both therapists, but our perspective on healing comes from two different worlds. She is very traditional and very logical in her approach. Barb's perspective is that if you can understand your issue intellectually,

A Dream    I had a dream about Barb the night before my session with her.

    I dreamt she was a bit frazzled about her family, in particular, her son. He was going through a difficult challenge that was affecting Barb and their whole family. In the dream, Barb was worried about him and his strength. Besides having "mom" energy, Barb is very forthcoming. As soon as I arrived, she shared with me that, indeed, her son was getting over a life crisis that had put her household in a bit of stress. I knew nothing of this consciously. I had not seen Barb for more than two years. This dream reinforced me to trust my instincts. We all learn differently. From my observation, Barb operates from almost pure logic, and I work from many diverse perspectives and levels of awareness. As with my sister, I did not reveal my dream to her. The dream was for me, for my growth.


then healing will ensue. I believe you can have totally different beliefs intellectually and subconsciously, and understanding something only intellectually will help you just so much. Even so, it felt so good for me to sob my little eyes out and have an objective, empathetic listener.

Quickly I came to realize that this would be my only session with Barb. I could sense dealing with this logically was not going to help me cope with Judith's illness and my old issues about cancer and death. I never told Barb how I felt. The session did help relieve some of the grief that was causing my physical symptoms, but I knew they would be back. Barb is kind-hearted and generous and wouldn't take money from me, so I sent her flowers instead. I thanked her sincerely and deeply. For me, just talking to anyone who had "mom" energy was nurturing and that happened too infrequently.

For the next couple of weeks, I tapped into my wonderful network of people who know alternative ways of physical and emotional healing. I felt I would know when a suggestion resonated with me, and soon one did.

My next help in dealing with my emotions came in the form of a process that deals with the subconscious mind. (Yeah! Finally, I felt I could get to the core of my grief.) You might wonder why I had a hard time finding a practitioner to help me. Honestly, I did not feel comfortable with the hypnotherapists in my area. I felt they did not have what it would take to get to the root issues with me. The process I decided on does deal with root issues and, like hypnosis, was a vehicle to help educate my subconscious mind to accept new empowering beliefs and facilitate letting go of old limiting beliefs and emotions that were hindering me.

My sessions went on for a few months. During this time I wept a lot and truly released my old grief and the unconscious hold it had over me. I knew was I healing because I felt myself being able to have telephone conversations with Judith without having to grit my teeth to stay calm or keep myself from crying. I also noticed that I was stronger and more composed after we finished talking.

One of the best results of the therapy was releasing the grief I did not even know I was carrying regarding Judith's leaving for the nunnery when I was five years old. I realized her sickness was bringing up deep-seated abandonment issues for me. Most people do not understand that energy from past trauma can be carried in your subconscious mind until it is truly released. Many times (like my situation) you might not know the energy from a trauma is still within you, until something in your present-day life triggers physical symptoms, like the dizzy spinning feeling I experienced, or depression.

I believe because I was willing to face Judith's journey with cancer head-on, I was given my own gift of healing. Part of my healing was letting go the last vestiges of abandonment and grief so I could to take one more step in learning and living from a more loving heart.

During this time, I went by myself to visit my sister for the first time since her cancer came back. I went out to see how Judith was dealing physically with the cancer therapy. Judith also wanted to put me on her bank accounts, in case anything happened to her before she made out her will. She asked if I would be the executrix of her estate, and I agreed with no hesitation. She was living in Carmel, California, and was renting a small cottage that

**The Rest of the Family**  You may be wondering about my other siblings. Well, two of my brothers had died years earlier. Max, the eldest, died of cancer. My brother Robert (remember the gun, and the bullet that almost killed me?) was an ultralight nut. (An ultralight is a hang-glider with a little motor. It can fly higher than a hang-glider, and you don't need to run off a cliff to fly.) Robert loved the sport so much he actually had a runway built in his back yard. He had a small-plane pilot's license and was really quite skilled in flying little planes. One day, after taking off from his back yard runway, he lost control, crashed in a cemetery near his house, and died instantly.

My brother Marty has not communicated with our family for about thirty-five years, and I personally think he suffers from paranoid schizophrenia. Besides Jean and me, there are my sister Joan and brother Michael. My sister Joan was not as close to Judith as I was; Michael was close but had many family and business obligations. He kept in touch with Judith, but Jean and I were her main emotional support in the family. Maybe it was a woman-thing, but Judith needed the female touch of just having someone listen to her and not try to fix her or tell her how to run her life.

was connected to a larger home.

During the first year of Judith's recurrence, my sister Jean and I did not do daily phone calls. As the disease progressed, our phone calls to Judith and to each other became a daily ritual. When I visited that first time, I did not have the daily calls with Jean to provide the strength I needed to deal with Judith and the ensuing business we needed to accomplish. I talked to my husband and my friend Beth when I was there, and that was comforting.

Judith was feeling sick to her stomach from the medications just part of each day when I was there. I remember one time we were in the parking lot of the bank and she had to stay in the car because of her nausea. Inwardly, I felt like a child again, taking care of my mother. It was a challenge for me to stay strong and clear of my old anchors of fear. The rest of the time we spent walking on the beautiful, scenic ocean trails that were near Carmel. We would walk for several hours and look at the sea lions and otters play and sun themselves. Most everyone in our family loves nature, and those walks were our main source of entertainment. I stayed only a few days, because both Judith and I had to get back to our businesses.

---

## FACING DEATH AND FEAR

Every time I talked to my sister and saw her in person I was dealing with my own fears of death and having cancer. One can be afraid of death and not even realize it. I have had a lot of spiritual experiences, so you would think I would not be afraid of death. I personally believe the fear of death is part of the human consciousness. Some people have little or no fear of dying—I wish I could say at that time I had been one of them. One of the numerous healings for me in helping Judith was a lessening of my own fear of death. I do believe when I face my fears I overcome them. My spiritual practice is one of deep growth for me and helping individuals through my coaching practice to live with more love and awareness therefore helps me stay focused on my own growth. The fear of death and other fears can keep you from living a fuller life, regardless of whether you want God in your life or not.

For example, when I was unconscious of my limiting beliefs and fears, I self-sabotaged my life with bad choices and relationships and kept myself from joyful experiences. Fear limits your capability. At one time I had a debilitating fear of people. I would get panic attacks, and being around people made me feel drained. Consequently, I did not socialize and when I was around people I kept a shield around my heart because I felt too vulnerable. (In my view, this was all due to my fear of death.) The more I was afraid, the less I allowed into my life; the more I released my fears, the more I permitted myself to accomplish and the more love and happiness I allowed into my heart. (This is just my belief. If you deeply analyze most people's fears you will find, at the core of them, the fear of death. Think about it.)

Through my dreams and my spiritual practice over the years, I feel I have been guided and helped to heal my limiting fears. I used to worry ninety percent of the time. Now my mind is at peace most of the time, even if things don't go my way. I am learning that my true self is Soul, and as Soul I am indestructible. Learning this is not an intellectual process. You can read about it, sure, but you have to integrate this learning into your very core. For example, you can read about Divine Love and meditate on it, but until you practice it with people in daily life, it is not complete; it is more theory than substance and reality.

Before the time I was facing my part in Judith's journey with cancer, God sent me other physical challenges to help me face my fear of death. When I was a child I could not tackle my mother's ill health with so much awareness. Most of the time I needed to be unconscious to survive, which was right for me as a child. As an adult and someone who has chosen to develop in this lifetime with awareness and Divine Love, I knew would have to confront death and tragedy head-on to eliminate my fear.

It started with my beloved cat, Foot. For seventeen years she was my dear friend, from the time I was twenty until I was thirty-seven. She was a black and white cat with extra toes on each paw. (Hence the name "Foot.") Foot was truly special. I believe, as many do, that higher mammals are also Souls; they are just having an Earthly experience with a furry body this time around. As with their human counterparts, some are more advanced than

others. Foot was one of the more advanced beings I have
ever met. When Foot looked at you it seemed she could
see right into your very being. Some people who met her
were put off by the powerful awareness that emanated from
her. She also had an incredible gift of healing. Foot could
sense sickness and depression and she would go right to
the part of your body that was hurt or in pain and lie on
it. If you were depressed she tried to wrap herself around
your head. After a few minutes you would feel better! It
was almost spooky.

Foot slept with me every night in the crook of my arm.
I would have very vivid dreams with her. Now I know that
some of these dreams were actual spiritual experiences
with this being of love named Foot.

After my first divorce, Foot got cancer of the liver. I
was truly devastated that I was going to lose my dear, dear
friend—to cancer, no less. After a couple of months dealing with her cancer, I realized that she was in great pain
and her quality of life wasn't good. I was trying to make the
extremely hard decision of whether to put her down. I
had never done anything like this before. The night before, I stayed up almost the entire night in spiritual contemplation. I was extremely conflicted whether I should
put her down. I knew Foot was Soul in a furry body and I
wanted to do right by her. Toward the morning, I received

inner confirmation that putting her down was the most loving thing I could do. The next day, I took her to the vet. I was with her, singing HU inwardly to her and sending her love when she passed. This was one of the most difficult things I ever did, as anyone who has put down a loved pet can attest.

Weeks went by, and I didn't dream of Foot. I really thought I would since we were so close. I wanted to know if she was okay. Well, about three weeks after her passing I was in session with a client. This client didn't know I had a cat. Part of my therapy and working with people involves analyzing their dreams, and this particular client started the session off by saying she had a dream about me. I asked her to relay the dream. She told me that in her dream, I was half-cat and half-human. As she related this, I started getting chill bumps on my arm. Next, she said I looked at her in the dream and smiled and said, "I am happy." I then asked my client what color the cat part of me was in her dream, and she said, "black and white." Just like Foot!

I almost lost it in that session. It took all my strength to hold back my tears. I had been so consumed with grief that I couldn't feel the love we shared, so my beloved friend had found a conduit to let me know she was safe and had moved on to a higher state of consciousness.

CHAPTER

4

# Animals Are Soul, Too!

A NIMALS ARE SOUL, TOO. MANY, LIKE FOOT, HAVE been my friend and teacher. I have always tried to communicate with my pets and other animals from a consciousness of Soul to Soul. These three powerful examples come to mind.

When Mark and I were first married, I found out I had to have a hysterectomy. Frankly, that scared me more than I'd like to admit, and I used all my spiritual and therapy tools to help me feel calm and positive. I knew I did not have cancer, but for me any surgery represented fear because of what I witnessed with my mom.

We had a cute little cat named Boo Boo at the time. As her name suggests, she was a "roundish," full-figured girl. Mark had found her before he met me. Boo Boo was crying by the screened porch of our (at that time it was his) house and had obviously been someone's pet because she was de-clawed and spayed. She was slow to physically bond with Mark and even after he adopted her, she never really let him pet her much.

Cats seem to always bond with me, so when I came to live with Mark, Boo Boo and I became good buds and she bonded almost exclusively to me. I love grooming kitties and soon Boo Boo let me brush her. After a while her eyes would light up at just the sight the cat brush. I had never had a cat since that liked being brushed as much as Boo Boo.

When I was dealing with my nervousness about my operation, Boo Boo started pulling out her fur. Cats will often do this when they are upset, but the trick is to find out why they are upset. Boo Boo was licking off her fur at the exact location of her uterus. I saw this and intuited she was picking up on my anxiety of having a hysterectomy. She was trying to deal with my fear and her apprehension for me, in her own kitty way. I told my husband what I thought was going on, and I told him I was going to have a "cat mom" talk with Boo Boo. Mark gave me the you-have-got-to-be-kidding look and wished me luck.

So I sat down with my furry friend and told her with both thoughts and words that I would be safe and come out of this operation healthy. I communicated sincerely to her not to worry, and I told her she could stop pulling out her fur, emphasizing I would be safe.

As it happened, the very next day she stopped licking off her fur. My husband was totally shocked, which (I should not admit) gave me great joy. I always knew Boo Boo and I were communicating; this was my actual proof.

A few years later, Zippity, another cat in our feline family, started to lick off her fur.

*I did not name our cats at this time. My husband, I must say, has a wit about him. When we adopted two gray sisters, he wanted a happy cat family so he named one Zippity and (you guessed it) the other Doo-Dah. Oh, the things one puts up with for love!*

This time I was clueless why our kitty was doing this. Mark and I were happy, and all was well in our life. I hated to see Zippity becoming bald; she normally had such a beautiful and luxurious silver gray coat.

Every night before I went to sleep, I would sing HU to myself and ask God for answers regarding Zippity's behavior. I had a dream after a few weeks of doing this. I dreamed I was having a conversation with Zippity just like you would with any person. She looked the same—big, gray, and a cat—but instead of mewing she had this high little voice and she spoke English.

I asked her in the dream why she was pulling out her

fur. She looked at me with her big eyes and told me she deeply missed our morning playtime. In the dream, I apologized to her for the slight. I got the awareness all was right with her now because she knew I understood and was going to play with her again.

When I woke up, I told her again that I loved her and that she could stop pulling out her fur, and I began to play with her. Like Boo Boo, she stopped her hurtful behavior immediately after I had this dream. And I kept my promise to play with her in the mornings.

Whether you believe it or not life is one big connection. Our energy and consciousness constantly affect people, animals, and the environment. I do not always remember consciously that my actions, thoughts, and energy affect the environment around me, but I try. I am not saying that individuals are responsible for others. All Souls, whether animal or human, are ultimately responsible for their own actions and reactions. When you live from a higher consciousness of love and care for yourself and others, without taking on their responsibilities, you can uplift life from your energy—your "being"—without interference or control.

I realized I was not responsible for our cats' pulling out their fur. But because I cared about them, I worked with Spirit to help them, without taking their responsibility. I was, in essence, teaching with love and communication. What they did with my teaching was their choice. The same holds true in daily life with our human friends and family. (This lesson became very important for me in dealing with my sister, especially as time went on and her disease progressed.)

Many times God or Spirit lets you know something is important with the cycle of three. I had three different cats with fur-pulling problems. The third was my cat Bear.

For years I conducted my hypnotherapy/success coach practice out of a traditional space in an office park. After about ten years, I bought a quaint, smallish house and worked with my local clients from there. After about a year in my new location this kitty, a little Maine Coon/ Tortoiseshell mix, came to my window looking to be fed. The house is a ranch, and the cat could look straight into the therapy room. If I had had more intestinal fortitude I would not have given her milk, but she looked so hungry. (Famous last words!)

I knew I was creating a problem by feeding this feline, but I was going away for five days so I thought she would convince another person to feed her while I was away. My belief was I could not have a cat living in the place where I conducted therapy. Wrong! After my five-day trip this little fur ball was still hanging out at my window, begging to come in by vehemently pounding on the screen. I was working with a client that day at the house. My client was facing the window, and Little Miss Persistent was beating away on the screen. She was not, I repeat not, letting up. My client looked at me and said, "I think you are being adopted!"

It was late fall and getting very cold at night. I was worried about this little cat surviving the cold temperatures so I decided to bring her in at night and look for a home for her. (So much for best-laid plans.) I named this kitty Bear, because she looked like a big brown bear and she could stand up on her haunches for a long time, just like a bear. Bear was a little defensive and independent from having been on her own for what I think was a long time. And oh, boy, was she smart! When I first brought her in the house I put her in the back bedroom. (I still thought my clients would think it unprofessional to have a cat in the therapy room with them.) Bear stayed in the back bedroom for all of an hour, consistently thumping on the door the whole time. I finally heard quiet. Yeah, I thought, she had accepted the bedroom. But no! Instead she managed to open the door. I found her in the waiting room schmoozing with my next client.

Bear loved people and the energy of the therapy room, and nothing was going to deter her from being where she wanted to be. I wanted her to have a good home so I found a person who was looking for a cat. Very quickly, I had discovered Bear nipped or bit a little when she was scared so I talked to her and asked her not to bite this person. I told Bear, through visualization and my thoughts, that this person might adopt her and soon she could have a new home—so behave.

Did she listen? No way. As soon as the woman approached Bear to pet her, she tried to bite her. The woman was aghast and declared (quite strongly, I might add) that "Bear was not for her."

My client—the one who witnessed Bear pounding on the screen—was right. Bear adopted me, and my clients benefited greatly from her love and energy. She soon turned into a loving being that welcomed my clients and soothed their nerves with her presence. We called her the "Wal-Mart greeter."

Remember, what I said about loving to brush cats? Well, after Bear had been living at my office for a while I tried to brush her, but she wouldn't have anything to do with it. Someone suggested I work with a little comb first so Bear could get used to the idea of that kind of touch. So diligently for several months I tried to comb her. I did this every day until she shook me off. This little one did not like being brushed at all, but I continued to try to train her into liking it.

One day I noticed she had started pulling out her fur. As usual, I brought this problem into my daily spiritual contemplation. I asked to be of service. If it was for Bear's highest good, let me know how I might help her to stop pulling out her fur. I was not attached to forcing my will on her. (Though looking back on it, I was a bit attached to being able to brush her.) I gently worked with singing the HU and let myself be guided by God.

∾ *Yikes, not another one! You might be wondering now, what I do to cats that they all want to pull out their fur? Nothing. It is just a method they have to communicate. I do want you to know I treat cats wonderfully. The cats that live in our house have it made—since I have no human kids, my cats are my four-legged kids. And I really hate to admit they do have my husband and me wrapped around their paws!*

After a few weeks, when I went to pet Bear I heard a voice coming from her as distinctly as I would hear a conversation with a friend. As soon as my hand touched her fur I heard her say, "I just want to please you." I got the whole meaning of what she said instantly, and I started to cry because she had such a profound love for me. She thought I didn't like her fur, because she associated the combing with removing hair from her body, not groom-ing. Bear wanted to make me happy and assist me in get-ting her fur off her body. What astounding love! Right there, with tears streaming down my face, I hugged Bear and told her how much I loved her fur and asked her not to pull fur off her body anymore. Over and over I told Bear in thoughts, pictures, and words how much I loved her fur and how much I loved her just the way she was. From that moment on, she never again pulled out her fur. And, of course, I stopped trying to comb and brush her.

These experiences with my cats showed me more fully how to work with other Souls without interference and even without words. I always asked God in my con-templations to see if I could help in any way. I asked for a solution for their highest good and the good of the whole. This way you do not interfere in another's spiritual growth or incur negative karma. These lessons with my cats pre-pared me for working with my sister Judith in the same spiritual, non-interfering way.

CHAPTER

5

# Back to California

I N THE SUMMER OF 2007, BOTH MY SISTER JEAN AND I noticed that in our phone conversations with her, Judith was even less forthcoming about her health and how she was feeling. Jean and I would call each other every time either of us had a conversation with Judith. When we talked with Judith, we each asked one or two questions about her health and noticed how she answered and reported back. Through this method, Jean and I got a fuller picture of Judith's health. Though Judith was guarded about what she was going through, inadvertently she sometimes would let a piece of information slip to either Jean or me. This was how we learned about the pain she was experiencing, what the doctors were saying, what her cancer markers were showing, etc.

Jean and I both believed her health was on the decline. So we decided to go visit her in California, thinking we would discuss with Judith her wishes for end of life care and what she wanted us to do with her belongings when she passed. Both of us intuitively knew not to speak to her about this before we saw her in person. Part of me was dreading the visit, while the other part was looking forward to being with both of my sisters.

Early November was a good time for all three of us and we planned our trip for a length of four days. Jean lives in Florida in the winter and spring and the rest of the time at her home near the Canadian border on the Saint Lawrence Seaway. Since we were going to travel together to California, Jean would have to connect in Atlanta, which for me was great.

The time for our trip was fast approaching, and I really wanted to send my sister Judith something to remind her how much I loved her. I truly thought her time for passing from this Earth was imminent. One day while Mark and I were walking in the mall near our home, I discovered the perfect gift for her: A Build-A-Bear stuffed cat!

*You know I am a cat lover; Judith and I traded kitty stories all the time. When I was a child I had a collection of about thirty stuffed cats. If Build-A-Bear stores were around when I was a kid I would have never left the store.*

Build-A-Bear stores are great. What makes their

stuffed animals unique, in my opinion (besides all the outfits you can dress your special friend in), is the way they
make the toy. You, the buyer, have to participate in building the toy. In essence you bring your special friend to
"life"! The store has special consultants that help you with
the process of building your new friend. First and foremost,
after you decide which kind of animal you want to bring
to life, you pick out a heart for it. The hearts are stored in
a big heart bin and then through a special ritual you
breathe love into the heart to make it real. Then you get
your stuffing and sew up your bear or cat or frog and choose
unique outfits for it.

Mark thought the idea was great and so authentically-
me. He knew the process of creating this toy would be hard
for me, so he asked if I would like him to go with me to
Build-A-Bear and be with me while I made the little cat.
I thought the idea of my big, strong, corporate husband
going to a children's store and helping me build my kitty
was a hoot!

We decided to go in the middle of the day because I
wanted as few people around as possible, because for me
this was almost a sacred mission. Too many strangers
around would, for me, diminish my undertaking.

When we got there a wonderful, kind person helped
us. I told the assistant about my sister and her cancer and

that this kitty was to be a very special gift for her. She understood completely, and she made Mark and me feel very cared for and comfortable. I proceeded to pick a spotted cat, and off we went to pick a heart. When I held the diminutive red heart in my hand, I wished my sister love, joy, and peace. It was all I could do to not totally break down in tears. I decided to name the kitty Angie, short for angel, because I wanted my sister to have an angel of love around her all the time. We stuffed Angie, put in her heart filled with love, sewed her up, and went around the store to find just the right clothes for her.

Since I wanted my sister to think of me when she saw the stuffed kitty, I decided to dress little Angie like me. So we got her a sparkly top, high heels, fashion pants, and sunglasses. Angie was "styling," as my good friend's teenager would say. Since Angie was too big to bring on the plane, I shipped her out ahead of our arrival. But I gave Judith explicit orders to not open the box until Jean and I arrived.

I met Jean's flight from Florida at the Atlanta airport and we flew into San Jose together and took an airport bus to Carmel. Neither Jean nor I wanted to mess with driving so we had arranged that Judith would pick us up at the bus terminal in the middle of town.

Jean and I talked a lot on the plane and caught up

with each other's lives.

We tried to form a game plane on how to approach Judith about the subjects of hospice and what she might want to do with her personal effects. We wanted to be on the same page and present a united front. Jean and I decided to play it by ear and wait for an opening during the visit that seemed appropriate.

The rest of the plane ride was uneventful, as all good plane rides should be. We landed and found the bus to Carmel, arriving at the terminal about an hour later. Judith was right there waiting for us. I cannot speak for Jean, but I know I was looking at Judith for signs of how she was really doing. On the surface she seemed strong and healthy and frankly, I was a bit surprised by how good she looked. We all hugged and piled into Judith's small car.

Without our knowledge, Judith had made reservations for us at this cute, comfy hotel and had paid for the rooms as well. Her place was just too small for us to stay there, and I think she wanted privacy. Judith was not a particularly social person and was not used to people being in her immediate space. Both Jean and I were quite taken aback by Judith's generosity, as she was always struggling with money. We tried to reimburse her for the rooms, but she wouldn't hear of it.

After we checked in, Judith walked us to our rooms.

We were greeted with two beautiful gift bags filled with chocolate (yum!), snacks, and a bottle of wine for each of us. This act of thoughtfulness touched both of us greatly. I was really blown away. After all, we came out to help and uplift her, not the other way around. I came to discover Judith would continue to surprise me with these kinds of thoughtful acts. Though she was the one who was sick, she continually was generous and thoughtful.

Jean and I decided to freshen up from our plane trip. Judith would come back later and pick us up. She wanted to show us her place and then all of us would go out to dinner. Jean and I had been traveling for over twelve hours, so it felt really good to take a shower and change and, of course, test out the chocolate. Judith returned about an hour and a half later.

We waited for Judith at the front of the hotel. When she parked I could see there was something in the front seat. With an impish grin she told me to take a look. Sitting there and looking as cute as can be was little stuffed Angie! At first I was disappointed Judith had opened her gift without my being there, because I wanted to see the look on her face when she first saw the kitty.

I said to Judith, "I told you not to open the box until we arrived."

She replied, "I did exactly as you told me. You arrived,

and I opened the box." (Talk about living the letter of the law when curiosity is getting the better of you!)

No matter, I had never seen her so joyful as when she received little Angie. Judith was beaming! She recounted when the box arrived several days before we got there, she could not imagine what would be in such a big box. Judith finally admitted her curiosity got the better of her and she just couldn't wait any longer to see what I had sent. When she opened the box, she told us she squealed and laughed out loud. She loved little Angie, and the kitty did indeed remind her of me. After seeing so much delight and pure joy in her face, I just couldn't stay disappointed.

The "four of us" went off to dinner. During our meal, I watched as Judith ate, gauging her appetite. She seemed to be eating pretty well, which made me feel a little better. In general she looked good. Her color, weight, and energy were fine. After dinner we went back to her modest bungalow. She was renting this small, yet charming one-bedroom cottage that was part of a larger property. After that, we called it a night and she took us back to our hotel.

## THE NEXT DAY

Jean and I travel well together. We have the same body clock, we like to do similar things, and we are the early risers in our family. Both of us were awake by four in the morning. (Our bodies were on still on East Coast time.) I waited patiently until the Starbucks across the street would open at five. Jean does not like their strong coffee, but I loved it at the time. I did my morning routine of a spiritual contemplation and then we got dressed and waited for Judith to pick us up.

Around seven we all went for breakfast at a locally owned restaurant that served absolutely the best breakfast food I have ever eaten. Though none of us are big breakfast eaters, the food was so fantastic that we all snarffed down everything on our plates.

<hr/>

## MY ADVENTURES WITH EMOTIONS

Since we are an active family Judith had planned a hike for the three of us at a nearby state park with beautiful, picturesque trails along the beach. At least we were fueled up for the hike. Judith was very diligent about being physically active and was walking daily to keep up her strength. And walk we did! We must have hiked a good two to three hours, watching the seals and otters play in the ocean and sun themselves on the rocks, as we trekked along the paths near the Pacific Ocean.

Toward the end of the walk, I started coughing. Little,

small coughs at first, like a clearing-your-throat kind of cough. As we continued, my coughing got worse and I could feel my throat starting to close down. I was getting really scared; I could hardly breathe, much less talk. My sisters were getting worried and honestly, I was starting to panic. We literally ran off the beach, and luckily we were near where we had parked the car. As I got closer to the parking lot and away from the beach, I could breathe a little easier. I no longer thought my airway would completely close down.

When we got to the car I suggested we go to a drug store so I could get an antihistamine. I thought I might have been allergic to something growing near the beach. After I took the antihistamine, I not only stopped coughing, I could breathe easier and I felt grateful to have my normal function of breathing return and my panicky feeling ease.

Judith's little place was the next stop on our agenda. She was worn out from the walk and wanted to rest. Jean and I suggested she take a nap, and Judith didn't argue. Jean and I, though, still had plenty of energy and decided to take another walk near Judith's place. (I said we are an active family!)

Jean made herself some coffee and took it with her for our leisurely stroll. There are some gorgeous hills behind where Judith lived so we decided to explore them. At the beginning of our walk was a back road with a big hill. About ten minutes into our walk and at the bottom of this big hill, my vision started to blur and I felt dizzy. I remember saying to myself, "I almost died this morning from not being able to breathe, and now I am going to die from a stroke." As calmly as I could, I told Jean I was dizzy and my vision was blurry.

She said in a panicked voice, "Why don't you just sit down for a while."

I then said in a much more panicked tone, "I think I may be having a stroke!"

Jean then turned to me and shoved her coffee, with artificial sweetener no less, into my face and commanded, "Here, drink this!"

I tried to be kind but I was scared and I replied not too kindly, "Are you out of your mind, trying to give me coffee when I feel this way?" I really did know she was just trying to help me in the best way she knew how. We both felt pretty helpless.

I tried to remain calm when I said, "Let me just walk slowly and see how I feel." I was afraid to sit down, I don't know why; maybe I thought I wouldn't get up again. So I focused my thoughts the best I could and breathed and walked slowly. I inwardly sang HU, though I did not direct it.

Very slowly my vision returned, and the dizziness went away. We gently walked back to Judith's cottage. To our surprise she was up and preparing dinner. When we told her what happened, she got upset that we didn't call her to come and get us. I tried to underplay the fear I had felt so Judith wouldn't be affected. I did not want to put any undue strain on her.

Frazzled from my two near-death experiences, I called my husband. I needed some reassurance and nurturing. I had to go outside to get cell phone reception, and I didn't want Judith to hear my conversation anyway. Thank God Mark was home and answered the phone almost on the first ring. After talking with him, I started to understand what had happened. Mark is my rock and grounding force; I jokingly tell him he makes it safe for me to be on this planet. We talked for a good bit. I told him what had happened and that I thought the two occurrences meant my suppressed fear and worry about my sister had surfaced as physical symptoms. He fully agreed with my assessment of the situation. Relief flooded over me when my logical husband agreed with me. I wasn't sick, just emotionally constipated. After I consciously realized this, I literally felt my body come into better balance.

I realized that seeing Judith had triggered my unusual

symptoms. Physically being in her presence, sensing her weakening condition, and feeling the need to remain emotionally strong made me suppress my emotions. That first day at her place, when she was showing us around, she looked at Jean and me in the eye and said, "See, I'm not dead yet, I look pretty good, don't you think?" Her saying that affected me greatly.

Although Jean and I had it in our minds to have the end of life conversation with Judith, when we got back to our hotel room that night, we both agreed we could not approach her yet about this subject. Throughout most conversations we had with her on this trip and for a good while later, Judith wanted everyone to focus on her healing. So talking about hospice, her will, and what she wanted to do with her worldly effects was not going to fly with Judith—at least not now.

A very subtle, but powerful way God communicates is through what people refer to as gut instincts or inner knowing-intuition. I know my inner nudge not to bring up hospice was God talking to me through feelings. Jean felt the same thing. For Jean and me, this intuition was confirmation on how to support Judith.

The rest of the trip went without any more bodily malfunctions for me, and for that I was extremely grateful. The remainder of our time we did the normal touristy

**The Highest Good**    I never visualized Judith well. I tried to remain neutral and ask for her highest good. Listening and being silent was the way I helped most of the time, even when she was instructing people to visualize her cured.

Everything in life is a spiritual journey. Everything. Sometimes hard experiences are what Soul needs, and sometimes the path or experience you need isn't anything you can even imagine or consciously want. For me, the easiest way to uplift my life and that of anyone I love is to ask for that person's highest good and the good of the whole. Spirit is always teaching; we are always dancing with God. You may not ever realize that. Many times I forget the real reason we are born and living on this Earth, also.

things—visiting the aquarium in Monterey, driving the coast highway, and touring the quaint, charming town of Carmel. Judith took naps every day. A couple of times we even ate out, but the last night we stayed in and cooked and watched a movie. We were bonding as sisters like we never did when we were growing up. As sad as the situation was, it was creating more love, caring and knowledge of each other's lives and bringing the three of us to a new, deeper level of relating.

CHAPTER

6

*Back Home Again*

O N MY JOURNEY HOME AND FOR MANY MONTHS AFTER,
I ruminated over life's turns and how really short life
can be. One moment you are a youth, next a young adult;
in a flash twenty years have gone by and before you know
it, the people in your generation are dying.

Most of the time I have felt somewhat different than
most people. I have always been a deep thinker and connected to life from a spiritual perspective for as long as I
can remember. Being this way has not been easy for me a
socially and consequently, I have not always felt connected
to my family or society as a whole.

In my first book, *You Are Soul*, I wrote in depth about
my childhood and the consequences of leaving home at
the young age of fifteen. Learning to navigate the world
and not succumb to the negative in life at such a tender
age was a Herculean task.

My brother Marty's nickname for me as a very young

child was "Sunshine." I remember having a very open and happy disposition until my mother got sick when I was five. Then I retreated into myself and found it hard to bond to my parents or brothers and sisters. I began to trust only my inner guidance, my intuition. This was not a conscious decision on my part. I was too young to make that kind of conscious determination to withdraw—it was a survival reaction. If it were a different time or if my parents had been more aware, I probably would have been given the counseling I really needed to help me handle the trauma of my mother's illnesses. Regardless, learning to trust my intuition and connect to God and the spiritual aspects of life at such a tender age has made me what I am today. And for that I am forever grateful.

Each child in our family responded differently to having an extremely ill mother. I may have not been the only "lost" child, but as the youngest, I definitely was extremely hard hit emotionally. Being a strong personality, I do not think my brothers or sisters knew how desperately I struggled just to be normal. Although I stayed in touch with different brothers and sisters over the years, I never participated in family get-togethers after I ran away at fifteen. Life for me then was about trying to survive on my own without parental guidance to fall back on.

## MY SPIRITUAL SCHOOL

As I look back now, I see that long period of struggle was my life-school of growth. It propelled me to investigate the meaning of life and my true nature as Soul. Over the years, I have worked diligently at overcoming my short-comings and fears. And I had many. I overcame a severe case of bulimia that plagued me for fourteen years. I also have suffered from and conquered panic attacks, social phobias, bad relationships, and very low self-esteem. Through inner work with my beliefs and emotional healing, I gradually found it easier to be around people without anxiety and without feeling like there was something wrong with me. Am I perfect? No. I know there is no perfection in life, but I definitely live now with more joy, love and inner peace. I really live life as a spiritual school, so I view the varied life experiences that are presented as opportunities for healing and growth.

## THE HAWAIIAN WORKSHOP

Shortly after I started my hypnotherapy/success coach practice I found out about this very exclusive workshop. It was to be held in Hawaii (yeah!) and its purpose was to help practitioners in alternative fields become better public speakers. Since at that time I was starting to promote

87

my practice through talks and I wanted to take my lectures to another level, I thought it would be just the thing to help my business.

The more profound reason I decided to attend was because of a deep urging, a nudge. I knew this was from God, though I didn't know what I was going to learn from this experience spiritually. When I got to Kauai and met the other participants, I found out the dynamics were exactly like those of my family. I was the youngest and there were four men and four women. (Well, that was interesting, more opportunities for me to heal family issues and I get to pay big bucks for it to boot. You just gotta love God's sense of humor!)

At that time in my life I was still quite anxious around people. With clients I was very confident, but in other situations my old feelings of being "less than" came to the surface, especially around people I perceived to be more successful or smarter.

To feel grounded or centered at that time, I needed a lot more time alone than I need now. Back then, being around people in social or learning environments mostly drained me. So a week of being with ten strangers (participants and instructors) was daunting to me. Sleeping quarters were shared, so I couldn't find solace in escaping to a private room. I was able to grab the only part of the room with a partition that could give me some semblance of privacy from the three other female participants, for which I was relieved and appreciative.

Eagerly I looked forward to doing my spiritual exercises every day on the beach in the early morning. I would find a quiet spot and sing HU and ask for insight and healing of my insecurities, and just doing the contemplations would bring me solace. The days were long and by the end of the week we all were feeling the pressure of the workshop and being around different personalities. Some tempers flared, but mostly we were all just tired.

One morning at the end of the week I did my spiritual exercises on the beach as usual. Usually I was the only person on the beach in the morning, and this morning was no exception. I tend to do my spiritual contemplations with my eyes shut, but that morning something prompted me to open my eyes. I had been singing HU for about five minutes and when I opened my eyes, I was stunned. In front of me were thousands—and I mean thousands—of little white crabs looking straight up at me and standing perfectly still. Through this amazing sight I could sense their reverence for the spiritual Sound, the HU.

Well, I closed my eyes as fast as I could and inwardly told them their form terrified me. You see, they looked like thousands of big spiders, and spiders have always frightened me terribly. (Not because they bite, but because of the way they look. For some reason spiders just scare me.) So inwardly I was petrified and at the same time realizing the crabs were honoring the HU, and telepathically I was asking them to go away because of my fear. This took all of a second. I immediately opened my eyes again after I communicated my message, and they were all gone! Poof, they had all vanished in the blink of an eye. Wow, I was floored! This is not how I had seen little crabs act.

I chose to keep this experience private; I realized it was a communication from God just for me. This incredible experience was a gift, a teaching, and a healing of my fears. Specifically, on this island and at this seminar, I was healing fear within myself that triggered embedded memories of hurts, real or imagined, from family members and others. As I was the youngest and least successful member of this workshop (or so I thought), every time I replaced my fear and inner shame or unworthiness with loving myself for my uniqueness, I grew spiritually and became happier. The whole workshop was a huge waking dream of healing and facing my fears. Seeing the thousands of crabs that looked like spiders and calmly singing HU and confronting my fears physically, was Spirit supporting me in my healing. This growth would later help me with dealing with my sister and her journey with cancer.

## LOVE AND HEALING

Spiritual growth is about accepting and giving more love in life. You are part of the whole that you need to love. Love is ALWAYS uplifting. As I tell my clients, love may not always look all warm and fuzzy, but may instead be an action that can be difficult to implement like developing and maintaining healthy boundaries. Think about it: having healthy boundaries prevents an individual from giving or receiving abuse or allowing negative encroachments from others. When you have healthy boundaries, you do the best you can to take care of yourself on every level. You respect yourself and others. Healing shame, feelings of unworthiness, and fears propels you to have more love in your life.

There are always family dynamics that can drive you crazy. In these situations I choose to look at how I can grow and be a better person from the experience. It is definitely not always easy for me to do that.

## COMMUNICATIONS FROM GOD

Communications from God direct my life and help me handle life from a higher perspective. I know my awareness at that moment is being uplifted and at the same time I feel inwardly supported and guided. We all have this opportunity whether we are religious or not. Living with the realization that God is indeed communicating to us all the time is learned. I became aware of this by observing life, doing daily contemplations, and not discounting my intuition and "woo experiences" (as my corporate husband likes to call them).

You may be having communications with God and be discounting them or not understanding that they are, indeed, spiritual in nature. One common way God uplifts us and communicates to us is through Spiritual Sound. Most religions talk about the Light, but very few talk about Sound. The Sound of God can be heard inwardly just by you or outwardly like my experience with the music I heard at my friend Beth's house. It can be music, thunder, a high single note like that of a flute, the buzzing of bees, or the sound of running water. This is the Holy Spirit talking to you.

Communication with God can be in the form of Light while you are contemplating or living daily life. It can take many shapes and colors. Many times I see a little blue star or a white star off to the side when I am working with a client. This tells me to pay attention to what we are talking about and for me to keep focused on the higher good.

Another way God speaks to you is through your dreams. Your dreams can be prophetic in nature, actual

Soul Travel experiences, or an easier way for you to confront your own issues. God is also talking and teaching us through what I call waking dreams. This is when you experience something in daily life that catches your attention or when someone says something that seems significant. Or when something that happens to you is out of the ordinary, like the white crabs I experienced in Hawaii.

A waking dream may also be something you hear that could be out of context or seem louder. When you hear this, your ears perk up and the message seems clear, though you might be the only one that "got" it. The more you attune your awareness of the different ways God is (indeed) communicating to you, the more you will experience it.

# Life Continues

THE HOLIDAYS CAME AND WENT IN A NORMAL WAY FOR me, but not for Jean. In January Jean's husband Ron was told the dreadful news he had prostate cancer. His doctor called him on his birthday with this information, no less. Once again cancer had come to our loved ones. After Jean and Ron got the doctor's report and had time to digest it, Jean called everyone in the family and told them. I was not completely surprised with the news, because Jean had mentioned her concerns on our way back from the trip from Carmel, saying she was worried Ron may have prostate cancer because his PSA number was high and that they would know for certain after more tests were done in Florida.

I cannot comprehend how Jean was able to handle all the emotions that must have been coursing through her during that time. She had a sister with stage-four breast cancer, and now her husband, and the love of her life, had cancer. Jean and Ron handled this crisis with action and aplomb. Ron researched his options of treatment, and Jean was incredibly supportive. They both remained upbeat and positive through the whole situation.

Soon after I heard the disquieting news, I remember a dream where I talked to Ron and asked him if he wanted my emotional support. Very calmly but firmly he said, "No, I just want Jean's emotional support." I am glad I had this dream, which I feel was a real inner communication with Ron. God again was helping me. Through this Soul Travel experience, I understood and respected Ron's decision for me not to get emotionally involved in his healing process and to leave that support to Jean, his wife.

## BOUNDARIES AND SUPPORT

I never purposely want to step over anyone's boundaries, even their emotional ones. Sometimes we can have the best of intentions, especially when we want to help someone, and end up crossing a boundary with that person.

Since it is impossible for anyone to know everyone else's boundaries, it is our individual responsibility to communicate and protect our own space. When you discover someone's boundary, it is up to you then, to respect it.

Boundaries can get very muddled when there is sickness involved, especially the life-threatening kind. Most people, myself included, are often guilty of offering our "wisdom," by making suggestions or telling others what to do. Most people's intention is to be helpful, but when we start telling others how to be or what to do without their permission or consent, we are interfering with their boundaries and space. When someone you know is going through sickness or a life crisis, the best thing you can do is ask, "What can I do to support you?" You also may want to ask them what they may want or need. Then listen, and follow through.

Jean and I tried to live this with Judith. Regardless of what we thought personally, we honored her wishes and her boundaries. We tried to live with the intention that her life was her life and she was on her own spiritual journey. What Judith needed was not necessarily what I would have needed, and vice versa.

Through a lot of diligent research, Ron found the treatment that resonated with him. In March he and Jean went to live near the Shands Medical Center in Jacksonville, Florida. They stayed there until the middle of May. Ron's cancer treatments lasted only ten minutes, but he needed to have the treatment every day.

Throughout the spring I focused on my business and my life with my friends and husband. Ron was doing

remarkably well, and Jean and I stayed in constant communication with Judith. Judith was intent on curing her
cancer, so Jean and I were very careful about asking her
how she felt. (We both thought if we did this would keep
Judith focused on the negative.) We each experienced
Judith's annoyance when we asked too many questions
about her pain level or cancer markers. Jean and I were
doing our own dance of non-interference and caring. We
got better at it as time went on, but it was very difficult at
times.

Toward the end of the spring, Jean and I extracted
more and more information from Judith. She started to
admit her pain was increasing and getting hard to man-
age. This was not looking good. (For Judith to say she was
in pain was monumental, because she could be quite
stoic.) She was having a difficult time eating certain foods
and her stomach was upset quite a lot.

In May of 2008, Jean and I became very concerned
about her. Judith's strength seemed to be failing and she
had to rely mostly on herself for everything. She could
drive in a crisis but she was isolated from help. Her friends
nearby were working and did the best they could to help,
and Jean and I were extremely grateful for them. Judith's
good friend Debbie lived about thirty-five minutes away
and was extremely conscientious about keeping in touch

with her, calling every day to check in on her. Eventually my sister's pain became debilitating and Judith told Debbie she decided to take an ambulance to her doctor to see what was going on. Debbie would hear nothing of that and stepped in and drove her to the appointment instead. After extensive and exhaustive tests, the doctor determined the problem was an infected gall bladder.

At that time Debbie was my only link to what was happening to my sister and I was in touch with Debbie almost daily. She acted as my sister's patient advocate and probably saved her life. Thank God she was there. I think most people feel helpless when a loved one is in pain and facing an operation. To be three thousand miles away and not be able to help was incredibly difficult.

My sister was admitted to the hospital on Saturday, and the doctor initially wanted to wait until Monday to do the gall bladder surgery. Debbie, acting as Judith's patient advocate, insisted the doctor operate as soon as possible. Judith, by that time, was delirious with pain.

Another problem besides the pain of the infected gall bladder was Judith's arrhythmia. This was occurring more and more often and it was rearing its ugly head again. Arrhythmia is when the heart's rhythm is very erratic and/or fast. Unchecked, can cause a stroke or a heart attack. When Judith would have arrhythmia, it completely drained her energy because her heart had to work so hard. Many times she reported it felt like she was dying from that, it was so debilitating to go through.

Her doctor was aware of that and he had to get the arrhythmia under control before he could operate. He was also contending with Judith having a high fever, probably due to the infection. Finally they got all the peripheral problems under control and the doctor did operate on her that Saturday, thanks mainly to Debbie's insistence. All day Saturday and Sunday I waited for the news of Judith's progress. Instead of sitting around the house on Sunday, I went out and played my usual golf game. (You may think that odd, but focusing so hard on each shot keeps me from worrying, so I knew I would not be overwhelmed by my emotions while I was waiting for news.)

It takes anywhere from three-and-half to four-and-a-half hours to play a round of golf. I still had not heard the results of Judith's surgery by Sunday and I played like I was in a fog (though I had a pretty good score, go figure). I kept my cell phone on me during the whole round. Several times I tried to reach Debbie about Judith's progress and because of the time difference and Debbie being in ICU with my sister, I didn't reach her until later that day. Debbie, I know, was extremely concerned. Judith was delirious and everyone who loved Judith was worried she would die.

Later Debbie confided that Judith asked her to go to her house and get her living will. Judith wanted the doctors to know she did not want to be resuscitated. Debbie got it, and when they were wheeling her down the hallway to be operated on, Judith signed the "do not resuscitate" order. This is how ominous and dire the situation was.

Toward the end of my golf game, I got a call from Debbie and she informed me Judith was recovering from the surgery, but was still extremely weak and that the last couple of days had been a harrowing experience. I still remember the call, club in hand, standing on the edge of a hill on the sixteenth fairway. Everything became a blur as I talked to Debbie about what my sister was going through.

After my game I talked with my husband, and we agreed I should go to California and help Judith with her immediate recovery. To accomplish this I had to cancel and reschedule my clients for the upcoming week and Mark sweetly offered me his frequent flyer points. As luck would have it, Delta had seats I could have with points on the exact days I needed them. For me this was another confirmation I should go to California.

After her operation, Judith had to stay in the hospital for a few days for observation. They wanted her heart to be beating without arrhythmia before they would let her go home. My timing looked like it would be absolutely perfect. I was going alone this time, as Jean and her husband were just returning from Jacksonville after many months away from their home.

I take a boatload of vitamins and supplements and I remember packing every kind of supplement I knew of to help with tension and anxiety. I kept repeating to myself, "I have to be strong for my sister." I knew it would be difficult to be alone with her, to have no one to confide in to relieve my tension. The last thing I wanted to do was to break down in front of Judith. I also knew I would have no privacy because I would be sleeping on the floor in her little living room to be near her to give immediate assistance should she need it.

## BACK TO CALIFORNIA

Without my sister Jean traveling with me, my flight was safe but lonely. By the time I got to California, Judith had been released from the hospital and was recuperating at her home. Debbie offered to pick me up at the airport, and then we drove to a Chinese restaurant where we would be meeting Judith for lunch.

In the hour or so drive to Carmel, Debbie and I had time to connect. She confided that the doctor told her that while he was removing Judith's gallbladder he had checked her liver for signs of cancer. (The usual progression of breast cancer when it metastasizes to other organs is to the liver, brain, bone, and pancreas.) The doctor did find small signs of cancer in Judith's liver. I was crushed. My dad died of cancer that had metastasized to his liver. It was an agonizing death. My emotions were in hyper-drive, and I was hanging on for dear life.

I was so incredibly grateful for Debbie. Though she lived thirty-five minutes away, Debbie was someone Judith really could count on.

Debbie and I arrived at the restaurant before Judith. I sat facing the door so I could see Judith as she entered. Debbie had warned me that Judith looked pretty bedraggled. When I saw her come into the restaurant, I cringed inwardly. She looked dreadful. Nothing Debbie had conveyed to me about Judith's condition prepared me for the shape my sister was in. She looked like she was on the verge of death.

As soon as we saw each other we rushed to hug, and both of us broke into tears. I didn't know what to say. Really, what can you say? Everything I was thinking seemed so trite or ineffectual. I ended up telling Judith I loved her and was there to help the best I could.

Judith's strength and determination always impressed me. Only a few days out of the hospital and on the brink of death, she was driving and going out to lunch. She looked like hell and she couldn't drive very far, but she was determined to be as active as she possibly could.

The three of us had a loving and tasty lunch, though my appetite was marred by the condition of my sister. I kept it to myself that I knew her cancer had spread to her liver. She reinforced over and over again that she wanted people to have only positive, uplifting thoughts about her and not think anything negative about her health.

༄ *I think I would have done something similar if I had to go through what Judith did. I teach and believe thoughts create. They are energy. I think it is difficult enough to deal with a major illness without having to deal with other people thinking of you dying.*

*For some people it may not be an issue. For someone sensitive like my sister, it is tremendously hard not to succumb to people's negative projections regarding cancer.*

After lunch, I drove my sister back to her place in her car. Judith wanted to rest, and I encouraged her to do so. I went for a little walk around her cottage and called Mark. It was so good to hear his voice. He has always been my grounding force and this time was no exception.

When my sister awoke from her nap she told me of

her struggles in the recent few weeks. I just sat, listened, and was her sounding board. Even though Judith was sharing her thoughts and feelings, I could tell there were many emotions she either didn't feel comfortable sharing with me or was out of touch with. I knew it was not my place to tell her what to do, even emotionally. I have an inner pact with myself: I never give advice unless I am asked, and then I tread lightly.

During the next couple of days, I met some of Judith's close friends and tried to gauge how I would discuss with Judith the handling of her earthly belongings when she did indeed leave her physical body in death.

It was problematical to mention the subject of dying because Judith was still adamant about focusing on curing the cancer. What I knew about it moving into her liver made me concerned about how much time Judith really had remaining. (At that time I was unclear if Judith knew her cancer had spread to her liver. I found out much later that she knew all along.) There were vital questions that Jean and I needed to address. Hospice was one issue. Another was how she would be taken care of when we were three thousand miles away, when she had no more energy and was in even greater pain. How would her bills be paid? Even though she had given me power of attorney and made me her executrix, at that time I had no access to her checking account and no way to pay her bills if she were unconscious. I had so many questions then and no answers.

All this and more was swirling through my head. I was trying to balance the basic, practical needs of my sister (who I felt was dying) and being an honest emotional support for her without telling her what to do. To say I was conflicted would be an understatement.

## BEING A CARETAKER

Many people who support loved ones going through major illnesses face these same issues. As the caretaker, whether you are physically near the person or not, there are so many aspects of concern. There are numerous levels of emotions you may contend with and may not even begin to feel until your loved one has died or recovered.

To the best of my ability I kept up my spiritual practice of singing HU and filling myself with Divine Love. I did this not only for Judith, but also so I could get through her journey without burning out and getting sick myself.

Those couple of days by myself with Judith were a test of compassion, patience, and tolerance. She was exhibiting impatience and the need to control. Her anger would surface, and I wouldn't know what triggered it. Pain, drugs, and the cancer (and, I imagine, living alone) were tremendously hard. As much as I understood this intellectually, when Judith became impatient or critical I had a hard time staying centered and neutral. Numerous times while I was there she would expect me to do things for her that she never asked for. Or she would criticize the way I did simple chores and she could come across frequently with a tone of irritation.

I remember going for a run while Judith took a nap the second day I was there. While I was away from Judith's house, I called Mark and just broke down and started to sob. I so wanted to be a loving and caring support for her. I did the best I could, as I believe Judith did the best she could, but the criticism was getting to me and I felt bad that I was letting it. Times like this are when supporters need help, like someone to listen to them about what they may be going through. As I tell my clients, I believe most women need to vent at times or we will literally explode.

Mark let me cry, really listened, and then reminded me of what I already knew. Judith was sick, just out of surgery, and coming out of anesthesia. These things affect one's personality. I knew he was right, and I felt relief to be validated. Being able to talk to him and have someone listen helped me to get grounded and become less affected by her aberrant behavior. Emotionally I felt as if I were going through a taffy pull. I had to dig deep for my inner reserves of strength and not get into a mindset of self-criticism when I thought I came up lacking.

When I got back from my run, Judith was feeling better and realized her behavior had been a little harsh. I kept my mini breakdown to myself because I did not want to burden her with my emotions. By that time, we were both better equipped to handle each other and the gravity of the situation. So I went about making her place sparkly and we talked about life and what spiritual growth meant to us. Judith had always been a spiritual "grow bunny" (this is what I like to call people who challenge themselves to grow spiritually or personally). She talked about confronting her karma and trying to live life as fully as possible, even with her health challenges, with the consciousness that everything presented in life is a spiritual lesson.

Judith wanted to live her life from purposeful, positive intention: for her and me, that meant living from the realization that all our actions create. So in essence, living spiritually means that consciously in each moment, through each experience, you live with awareness of how you want to act and react. Remembering to act in ways that produce the most love, uplift life, and connect to God and to not react as a victim or negatively is our version of living with a spiritual consciousness. Though Judith and I had different spiritual paths, we agreed on many things.

On the last full day of my visit, I was able to approach the subject of actually physically taking possession of at least some of her checks, so if she became unconscious I could pay her bills. This may sound small and insignificant, but for my incredibly independent sister to relinquish control (or even partial control) of her money to me meant she was realizing she could die at any time.

To my relief, I did accomplish this before the end of my trip. Judith did let me have one and only one check. That feat, in my mind, was monumental. I left for Atlanta with more peace of mind that I could help Judith if she had a crisis, but with a little more resignation that Judith's disease was winning.

CHAPTER

8

# Relationships

I GOT BACK TO ATLANTA TOTALLY EXHAUSTED. MARK and I had booked an Alaskan cruise months earlier and the timing of it couldn't have been better. (Well, to be completely honest, I booked the cruise and Mark agreed to come.) We were to leave for the cruise about two weeks after my return from California. I was especially looking forward to the cruise; for most of my life I have had a deep longing to go to Alaska.

I am much more of a nature lover than my husband, and I knew this trip would stretch his patience. ("Bless his heart," as they say in the South). Mark enjoys visiting cities more than the great outdoors. I can take pleasure in both, but the outdoors soothes my Soul. And I most definitely needed a trip to nurture my Soul. To his credit, Mark was a good sport and he kept his whining down to a minimum. He really knew how much I needed and wanted this trip.

## SPIRITUAL RELATIONSHIPS

If you examine our relationship, on paper Mark and I look like total opposites, but our values and tastes are quite similar and, most importantly, we complement each other. We have both become better people from knowing each other, we laugh every day, and the majority of the time we have an abundance of joy.

To me this is a spiritual relationship, one that stretches you toward being the best person you can be. It is not always easy and doesn't always look like you might think. In a committed relationship, I believe you do not have to have the same religion or spiritual path to grow spiritually. It took me a long time to come to that realization. (Two divorces, to be precise.)

My first two husbands were good people. We even practiced the same religion and spoke and understood the same spiritual language. That being said, they were not, however, what I needed to grow for my highest good in this lifetime. Through these relationships I learned tremendously while I was healing and clearing old karmic debts for myself and for them.

After my second divorce, I chose to take an even more intense look at myself. My life was not reflecting what I wanted with regard to relationships. I very much wanted a loving, joyful, committed marriage. I teach that your outer life is a reflection of what you truly believe consciously and subconsciously, and that the emotions you have not dealt with absolutely affect you. After my second divorce, I choose to deal with the beliefs or emotions that I knew must be blocking me from having the relationship of my dreams.

Since intellectually I believed I wanted and deserved a great relationship, I had to delve deeper into my subconscious beliefs and emotions to ferret out what was blocking me from having a healthy, committed relationship. See, your intellect is just ten percent of your mind's power, and your subconscious mind is ninety percent. You can have totally different beliefs intellectually and subconsciously. One way to understand this is when you know what to do and you don't do it. Or when you keep experiencing obstacles to your goals, like I had with my marriages (and, frankly, every romantic relationship I had until I met Mark).

Many of my clients have tried many different styles of coaching and therapy and have been unhappy at the lack of progress. When they change their underlying negative and limiting subconscious beliefs and emotions, through the work they do with me, they are astonished at the progress they make and how easily they achieve their goals. Like my clients, I had to do the same thing if I wanted a happy, fulfilling relationship. One reason I believe I am a good therapist is that I try to walk my talk. I have overcome numerous things in my own life, and my clients really relate to me because of that. I feel this gives them courage to confront whatever issues they may have in their lives.

## SPIRITUAL GOAL SETTING

That year after my second divorce, over the Fourth of July holiday, I went to a spiritual seminar in Minneapolis. It was similar to a retreat, but more active with classes and uplifting music and personal stories. The whole purpose of this kind of seminar is to help you strengthen your connection with God and Divine Love so you can live your daily life from a higher consciousness and create a greater ability to love and be loved.

At the seminar a workshop on spiritual goal setting lit up for me. The class emphasized goal setting in the context of living with the spiritual end in mind. Many books out now teach you to visualize what you want, but they leave out or don't teach that the true meaning of this life is spiritual. To have goals without a profound or more loving end in mind can be detrimental to you from the higher viewpoint of your growth as Soul. Your mind does need to focus, and will, but what you focus your mind on will open you to Divine Love or not.

In the workshop I learned I needed to ask for goals for my highest good and the good of the whole of life. Thy will be done, in essence. Letting go of attachment to actually getting what you want is the key. Now that may sound contradictory. But imagine putting your objective into the hands of your Spiritual guide or of God, and asking for your highest good for you, as Soul. The result will emerge for your highest good, though what happens may not be what your ego wants, but then again it could be.

*This is not the only physical lifetime we experience. As Soul we reincarnate. I am not saying you have to believe as I do. If you do, I hope you realize a more profound comprehension of how important this particular lifetime is for you. If you don't, I hope this information starts you thinking about the myriad of possibilities this life could hold. If you get trapped into the dance of Earth only, focusing exclusively on the minutiae of daily living, you limit realizing the more profound purpose here for your lifetime—that your real true nature is Soul. This is important because everything of an Earthly nature ends. You as Soul are eternal.*

During that seminar, I vividly remember taking the

class and making an inner vow to myself, my spiritual goal. I asked to face whatever I needed to face within myself that has kept me from a loving, joyful, committed relationship. I was completely serious about that statement. Since all growth and accomplishing goals in life starts within the individual, I knew my commitment would accelerate my spiritual growth, whether or not I found a relationship. Through clearing old limiting beliefs and emotions, and connecting more clearly to God each day, how could I not be better off?

After the seminar I came back with total determination and a clearly defined game plan to accomplish what I needed to learn.

## MY DATING SCHOOL

Every day I did a spiritual exercise to free myself of childhood issues I had with my parents and men in general. A spiritual exercise can be as simple as singing HU or visualizing Divine Love entering your heart, releasing old negative and limiting thought patterns. I also began my outer actions—what I called my dating school. Since I do not go to bars, I don't work in a corporation where I could be exposed to available men, and my friends didn't know any single men, I had to be inventive to meet available men.

This was just before Internet dating. One day when I was bored, I picked up a local paper and saw an ad for a telephone dating service. It was very affordable, and I thought, "Why not?" So I got right to work and put my voice mail ad in the system. This was the beginning of what I call My Year of One Dates.

Since meeting single men this way was new to me and I didn't know what to expect, I met all the prospective dating candidates for coffee at Starbucks and never gave them my home number. Also, I didn't want to meet them for a meal since, if we did not hit it off, a cup of coffee was a lot faster to get through than lunch or dinner. Being a realist, I understood everyone I would meet was not going to be a spectacular conversationalist, much less a romantic connection.

I approached the dating process with the intention of learning about myself regarding what I really wanted and liked in men, whether or not I ever met "Mr. Right." I realize that sounds so elementary, but I had never been in a healthy place in my life before regarding relationships, and I had gone about dating in a needy way. (Heck, to be perfectly honest, I never dated. I just got married, but I digress.)

Through the way I went about this dating process, I empowered myself. I discovered what I needed and allowed myself to receive what before I thought was impossible. Besides dating new men, both my ex-husbands reentered my life, and I cleared up what I believe to be the last of my karma with them.

## A WAKING DREAM

Spirit teaches in many forms. One form, as I have mentioned before, is the waking dream. This is when something happens in your daily life that is very much like a sleeping dream, but you are awake. A waking dream is a message you recognize for yourself through an occurrence.

I knew I was making progress when I had this entertaining waking dream. I was driving on the expressway around Atlanta and I noticed two cars side by side in front of me. I observed the first car had a Life Chiropractic College sticker on the rear bumper, and the second car had a Canadian flag sticker. (My first husband went to Life Chiropractic College, and my second husband was from Canada!) What was even more amazing was that when we came to a fork in the highway, I went in one direction and BOTH of the other cars went (together) the other way. To me this was a waking dream that signified my karma with these two Souls was finished. (I also like puns and karma sound very much like "carma." Get it?

Whether you got the humor God sent to me is not the issue. It spoke to me. That is how waking dreams work. They are your personal direct message from God.)

## MEETING MARK

That experience occurred in the spring of the year after I attended the spiritual seminar. During my daily spiritual exercises a few days later, I had an absolute inner knowing that the relationship I wanted was established. It felt like something went "pop" inside me, and I said to myself, "I have the relationship." I felt totally calm and at peace. There was no internal voice anxiously wondering if or when I would ever have a great relationship: I had complete conviction it would happen, no matter what. Now I have to admit, being a being a normal, red-blooded, woman I did ask God, "So when, already, am I going to meet him?"

After that "pop" I immediately started having a series of dreams that showed me the energy of the relationship and a little of how the man would look. The dreams also conveyed that it would manifest soon. I kept doing my One Dates and I met some really nice people, but felt no romantic connection. Until I got a call from Mark, that is. He sounded smart and witty on the phone, and we seemed to have great rapport.

So we decided to meet. No Starbucks for us, we were going to dinner. Yikes. I had a feeling I would have fun, and as it turned out I was right. I ended up marrying him a few years later. Significantly our first date was exactly one year (to the day) after I made my inner commitment at the spiritual seminar. It was the fourth of July. We got married seven years later on the fourth of July. After two divorces I just didn't want to rush into anything.

## RELATIONSHIPS AS GIFTS

Relationships can be vehicles of tremendous growth if we take advantage of the gift. Even disagreeable relationships mirror back to you what you may need to look at within yourself, and they can teach you compassion or neutrality or Divine Love.

My relationship with my sister Judith was not always easy, even though we had great affinity and loved each other. As time went on it got problematical for me to handle my grief and provide her neutral support, but I did the best I could. I am sincerely appreciative that I had my husband and friends for my anchor and support. From helping Judith, I know from personal experience that people who are assisting others also need support.

For a year after her gallbladder was removed she felt wonderful. Judith continued with her work, conducting seminars, writing, and training interns to do the work of her Mandala process. Her Mandala workshops were her way of teaching people the more profound meaning of life through art processes and meditations. She was blessed at this time with energy and very little pain.

Our daily talks were mostly upbeat and positive. Judith was focusing on completely beating the cancer. She never revealed to anyone in the family her cancer had spread to her liver, and I never mentioned I knew. I figured if she wanted me to know, she would have told me and I can only conjecture why she didn't confide in either Jean or me about this. My thought was she didn't want to burden us. More importantly, she wanted everyone to keep focusing on her defeating the cancer. I kept remembering my pre-monition dream—the one where the lady came running to me for help and my house slid off its foundation. I couldn't help but wonder if that dream had also revealed Judith would die. My dreams have always educated and aided me. I view premonition dreams as God's way to help your lower bodies, the mind and emotions, prepare to deal with an upcoming situation.

Regardless of what the future might bring for Judith, I kept bringing my attention back to the present. The eter-

nal now, the present, is the only time any of us have. I had
to remind myself of that over and over again. I chose to be
of service to my sister. For me, that meant helping her in
any way I could, emotionally and physically, and holding
the intention for her highest good spiritually without
losing myself in the process.

Judith taught many of the same things I impart
through my client sessions, albeit through her classes and
workshops. Part of her personality was exacting and de-
tailed. When she was not teaching, she could, at times,
come across as didactic. Her intent, I think, was always to
uplift, but at times I really struggled with not telling her I
already knew what she was saying. She needed, I believe,
to talk and have someone listen to her. I made a vow to
myself not to get into an ego battle with her. My spiritual
lesson was to come from my heart, not the ego. This was
in no way always easy to do.

The holidays came and went again. Jean's gift for the
holidays was her husband's clean bill of health. The treatment for his prostate cancer was absolutely the very best
for him because he had no side effects and he felt great.
This was such wonderful news, especially considering what
usually happened in our family when anyone got cancer.

Because Judith was eating a more vegetarian diet, for
Christmas that year I sent her my homemade white pep-

permint candy and some wonderful dried vegetarian soups. I figured she didn't need more material stuff, but great tasting food is always welcome. Jean and I were becoming more steadfast at listening to what she said and how she sounded at this juncture, because time was ticking away.

# Judith Moves to Oregon

JUDITH COULD STRETCH A DOLLAR FURTHER THAN anyone I know, but she had always had financial struggles. She confided to Jean and me that living in Carmel had become too expensive for her. Judith was always looking ahead, wanting to live in a place that would nurture her abundant creativity, be a beautiful, natural setting, and be affordable. Now more than ever, she also needed to live near people she could count on. She had only one or two people like that in Carmel and they didn't live nearby. Another thing that concerned her was that she had to drive to get any place she wanted to go. She was looking for a community of like-minded people in a smaller town environment. Around January, Judith started in earnest to investigate new places to live.

My sister was very practical and independent. Jean, our brother Michael, and I all offered to have her live in our homes, but to no avail. Judith also was not used to living with anyone and being a contemplative, creative type, she needed lots of alone time and plenty of space. Jean and I intuitively understood this and never pushed her to live with either of us. Regardless of how the disease would progress, we knew it was Judith's life and she was totally in charge of her choices. Only she could know what she wanted and needed.

## JUDITH'S NEW HOME

She eventually found the perfect fit in the little, creative, and bohemian town of Ashland, Oregon. Ashland is located in a little valley where you can see the mountains from the town center. It is famous for incredible theater. It has several top-notch playhouses and people come from all over the country to see the summer productions. Ashland has about twenty thousand people in constant residence and a multitude of great, diverse restaurants and coffee houses. It exudes creativity and its residents are friendly and eco-minded. Judith moved there in July of 2009.

For moving somewhere new, Judith knew quite a few people in Ashland. She had met several people through her work and travels and they, in turn, introduced her to other people. To her great relief and joy, she had an instant community and social network. The town was small enough to get around without a lot of driving, and as we later came to know, the people there were loving and down-to-Earth. Judith never had that kind of community in Carmel. As beautiful and quaint as Carmel is, it is still very spread out, larger than Ashland, and the people were harder to get to know. Her rent in Ashland was half of what she had been paying in California, and the place she rented was almost twice as big. It was also within walking distance to the center of town.

Another thing Judith loved about this small town was the park. This park is quite large, gorgeous, and located right off the main street, and it has duck ponds and walking trails galore. Being able to take daily walks was very important to my sister, and having a lovely place to walk was equally vital.

Jean, Judith, and I kept up our daily ritual of telephone conversations. A big hurdle for Judith was finding all new doctors. She interviewed different doctors and asked people she knew for advice. She was looking for doctors to help her with pain management who would also respect her way of dealing with her cancer.

Judith had decided to go totally alternative because the normally prescribed medications for breast and bone cancer caused her severe reactions. Any drug they gave her to help stem the growth of the cancer caused her either debilitating pain or intestinal problems. Judith's focus was still curing the cancer, if she could, without compromising her quality of life. It is very difficult for most people to trust their own inner guidance as to what is right for them, even when they feel strong and healthy. Judith chose to trust her inner guidance when she was sick, and not just with any sickness . . . cancer. She was a profoundly strong-willed individual and she absolutely walked her talk. Judith took full responsibility for her life, regardless of the socially or medically accepted norms.

Just saying or hearing the word *cancer* strikes fear in most people. It is so easy to shut down and let others take control and tell you what is right for you when you are scared or sick. Part of the spiritual journey is to learn the lesson that each person, each Soul, is absolutely responsible for his or her life, emotionally, mentally, physically, financially, and spiritually. What may be right for you may not be right for me; to know that is easy, to live it is another story.

During our phone conversations, Judith told Jean and me about her search and how she confronted (with dignity, I might add) the doctors and discussed how they might work together. She eventually found a great team of doctors that respected her and how she wanted to approach her healing.

## JUDITH BECOMES RAJITA

Before she moved to Ashland, Judith confided she was going to change her name to reflect her religious beliefs. Her spiritual path was now Hindu and she followed the teaching from a temple in Kauai, Hawaii. The main tenets of this sect of Hinduism are: your true identity is Soul, not the body; you are responsible for your life; your present life is but one of many lifetimes of learning; and respect that each Soul has its own path back to God. I live my life from these same beliefs. After a lifelong search, my sister finally found a loving, spiritual group she could relate to that was of solace for her, and for that I was very happy.

She picked the name Rajita, which means luminous or filled with light. To change her name, she would have to go to the temple in Kauai and participate in a special name changing ceremony. The ceremony would probably take place at the end of that year.

I remember I was driving in my car talking to Judith on my cell phone (yes, I know that's not a safe thing to do) when she told me about changing her name. I reacted with neutrality. I wanted to see her happy and at peace, and if this made her happy, great! As Shakespeare wrote in *Romeo and Juliet:* "A rose by any other name would smell as sweet." Judith would be my sister no matter what she changed her name to. When she told me the name she picked I actually liked it better than Judith.

When I was a child all the siblings called her Judy. When she was a young adult she wanted everyone to call her Judith, probably because she wanted people to take her more seriously. I personally think Judy is a happier, bouncier, more approachable name (especially for my so very serious sister.) Calling her Judith made me feel I was speaking to a very strict schoolteacher. But I do believe others can carry off the name Judith and not leave people with that same impression.

During that spring she still hadn't told anyone else about her decision to change her name and asked me to keep it confidential, which I did. I think she was getting used to the idea and would share the news with others if and when it felt right. In our Western society, changing your name for spiritual reasons is a very difficult and un-usual thing to do. It takes conviction and strength to live your life authentically, especially if what you do is differ-ent or runs counter to the norms of society.

Shortly after Judith told me about her wanting to change her name she told Jean. Jean, predictably, was also very accepting of Judith's new name. Jean's nature is one of tolerance and acceptance of people and their uniqueness. This is something I admire greatly in my sister Jean, and my respect for her qualities only got stronger as time went on.

＊＊＊

## ANOTHER WAKING DREAM

Remember me telling you about waking dreams? A waking dream is some happening in your life that you know or sense is a message from God.

Well, in April of 2009 Mark and I were watching a DVD in our movie room when all of a sudden we heard a boom! It was the loudest noise I have ever heard in my life, and it sounded like a jet had hit our house.

It had been raining exceptionally hard, and Georgia is known for intense thunderstorms. Mark and I looked at each other and said at the same time, "Our house has been hit by lighting!" We catapulted out of our seats and ran up two flights of stairs (our new kitten Sam thought this was a new game and great fun and raced us to the top of the stairs), expecting to see our house on fire.

We inspected the whole house and, to our relief, found no structural damage and no fire. Upon further scrutiny, Mark found his computer, the life-blood of his business, was fried. All of his information was saved remotely, but he could not get on the Internet. This was unfortunate, but not crippling. He ended up buying a wireless router and within hours he was back on-line. Over the next week, though, we found the lightning had zapped our freezer and our upstairs air conditioner. Luckily we were under warranty for the air conditioner and the cost to fix the refrigerator was manageable.

After a few months went by, I realized the lightning strike was a waking dream from God, preparing me for the year to come. I did not immediately know what it meant, but I sensed God was talking to me.

This lightning strike was particularly significant because it occurred on the first day of a springtime spiritual seminar I usually go to. For me this was no coincidence. God talks to us through Sound and Light. Lightning, with the consequential thunder, is sound and light.

I realized this waking dream was helping me see my old frozen thought forms (the freezer) would be melting away with some costs, but manageable costs. My emotions would be tested and helped (air conditioner under warranty), and new ways of assimilating beliefs or awareness would come my way (the wireless router).

---

## MORE TRYING TIMES

I was really tested and stretched in 2009 to live from a greater connection to God. Nothing on this planet lasts. The only non-change is change. This was the year of the

| Spiritual Growth | Spiritual growth does not come into your life directed by your ego. Higher growth comes by handling life, no matter what comes your way, from the consciousness that each experience, each occurrence is a spiritual lesson. A great thing to do to help you achieve this in |

daily life is ask yourself, "How can I grow in Divine Love from this incidence" or "How can I be a more direct channel for Divine Love right now?"

When you approach life with this attitude your heart does indeed connect with God, regardless of your life's circumstances. It is not always easy, especially when you are faced with a change that entails sickness, death, or financial loss.

incredible stock market crash, housing market drying up, and huge loss of jobs. It was an amazingly trying time for me, the most difficult I can recall since I ran away from home at the age of fifteen. I lost a big chunk of my savings (as did most of the world), my business was soft, my sister had stage four cancer, I had to put our cat Zippity down in May, and if that wasn't enough to handle, I got into a horrendous golf cart accident on the fifth of July (which, coincidentally, is my sister Jean's and my sister Joan's birthday).

I think I am the only person for whom golf is a contact sport. My accident was like something out of the movie *Caddyshack*. I was playing the best round of golf of my life when I got smacked. The day of the accident, my husband Mark didn't feel like playing golf and went to the gym instead. I got paired up with a lovely couple, Brian and Diana, whom I had not met before. I was alone in a golf cart and zipping along, making long drives, birdies, pars, playing the best golf of my life and wondering who the heck was this golfer—I had never met her before, but I liked her and wanted to see her more often.

On the seventeenth tee box, and before I teed off, I called Mark. I told him (actually I squealed, but in a golf-subdued voice) that I was having the best round of my life and I would be home in about fifteen minutes, since we lived right off the golf course.

July in Atlanta that year was exceedingly hot and dry. It hadn't rained in a few months and the sun had baked the ground. We had started the round early, around seven-fifteen in the morning. By the time we got to the seventeenth tee box, it just started misting. This tee box is exceptionally steep and high. It is situated on a small cliff overlooking the green. After I hit my ball, I got into my golf cart and started following the other couple down the winding, asphalt golf cart path. They were already at the green when my cart hydroplaned out of control on the slick, wet surface. Instead of slowing down, the cart sped up and hit the edge of the grass and path. The whole cart tipped over, pinning my right leg, and trapping me facing sideways under it. I vividly remember clawing the air, trying to grab hold of something, anything, because, I felt (and was) totally, wildly out of control and had no way of stopping this incredibly heavy vehicle. My right leg was completely trapped under the cart and I was being dragged on the asphalt with the golf cart on top of my leg.

I finally came to a stop after about fifty feet, trapped with the golf cart still on top of me. I started yelling at the top of my lungs for help. I wish I could say that being the spiritually orientated person I am, I had lovely thoughts and my attention in my time of need was on Spirit—no way, not this time. I was terrified, probably in shock, and all I wanted was to get the cart off me and see if I was paralyzed or not.

Brian heard my screams. (Actually I believe all of the golf course could hear me scream.) He ran over and tried to lift the golf cart off my leg. He couldn't. I continued to encourage him with my strident, out-of-control screams, "to get this cart off me." He took my intensely forceful verbal encouragement to heart. After five or six tries he managed to lift the incredibly heavy golf cart high enough for me to get my right leg out from under it.

To my massive relief I could move every part of my body. No bones were broken and no torn ligaments—quite a miracle in my estimation. At that moment I knew I was protected. Something should have broken; I could have been paralyzed or killed. My leg was at a twisted angle, and from the kneecap down was bloody and black with third degree burns from the friction of the cart dragging my leg over the asphalt. By now some one had called 911, and I was handed a phone to call Mark. On the phone, weeping, I told him what had happened. Two minutes earlier I had told him I was coming home with a great score, but now I was a mess. He asked if anyone was helping me and how I was doing. I told him all I knew. Mark told me he'd meet me at the clubhouse right away.

Another golfer friend came from another fairway to help. Keith drove me to the clubhouse in another golf cart. Waiting for me there were Mark and an ambulance. I was put in the ambulance, with fifty or so shocked golfers staring at me, and taken to the emergency room. Mark followed me to the hospital in his car. I was x-rayed and cleaned up and sent home. My leg was a mess. It had so many bandages on it that I looked like a mummy from my knee to my ankle. I thought my skin would heal in a month or two, but that turned out to be wishful thinking. It took over a year and a half. I was in bandages for seven months and the first ten days of my injury cost over five hundred dollars in bandages and ointments alone.

That year I felt pummeled on every front. I tried my

best to stay centered and discover what I needed to learn from a spiritual perspective. Even through all of this I kept saying to myself, "I need to be strong for my sister Judith." I was bone tired. My injury was not life threatening, but it drained my reserves of energy and inner peace.

I kept going to work because I had my own business; I could not afford the luxury of not working. My business suffered, as I had no energy for two-and-a-half months.

One technique that got me through it all was to mentally stay focused in the present moment. Fear is really about the future that may or may not come, and anger is usually about the past. When I focused my attention on the ever-present now, I had more energy and strength.

---

## A CHANGE FOR JUDITH

Judith remained adamant about focusing on her getting well up until the fall of that year, when she unexpectedly started to talk about getting palliative care, which meant treating the pain and keeping her comfortable, not curing the cancer. This was a one-eighty in her focus, and it took Jean and me by surprise. To this day Jean and I do not know what happened to cause her to admit to others that she was, indeed, dying. We have speculated some cancer marker came back high, or perhaps intuitively she just knew. More tumors were growing now, in her neck and jaw. They did not interfere with her ability to talk, but I am sure they caused her to realize she was losing her battle.

She contacted the Temple in Kauai where she was a member and scheduled a time in the late fall to go through the name change ceremony. Judith would be there for ten days and would be accompanied by a friend of the same religion, so Jean and I felt she would be taken care of. Her arrhythmia was manifesting more frequently, and this was our major concern at this juncture.

Judith, now Rajita, came back from Hawaii with a wonderful energy of peace, even though she experienced several bouts of arrhythmia while there. In a photograph taken at the time of the ceremony, her beauty and inner peace just radiated through her countenance. I believe it was the best photograph of her in her life! My sister Jean thought so, too.

---

## MY CHRISTMAS GIFT TO RAJITA

Christmas and the holidays were fast approaching. I knew this would be Rajita's last Christmas. The only thing I could think to get her was a letter that expressed what her life meant to me. This is the letter I sent her in 2009.

*My Christmas letter to you, Rajita!*

*So rarely do we tell the people that we are close with, how much they have meant to us. So I am going to do this for your present this year (as well as some peppermint candy:).*

*Ever since I was a little girl, I have always looked up to you and not only have seen you as my special big sister, but you were more of a mother to me than our Mom. I remember very clearly now that when you left for the nunnery I was devastated inside. I had no words at that time to express my loss so I just retreated inside. I remember looking down from your room and sitting on the wooden built-in desk and wondering why you were leaving.*

*Being able to visit you in Montana and North Carolina gave me strength to carry on somehow. I think Dad must have known this, as he was always very open to me visiting you and paying for the plane trip, which for Dad was a little out of character.*

*Through your artistic creative energy, you taught me how to access my own. You let me into your life and shared yourself with me in many ways, through the little meals we had in your kitchen in Sausalito, when I'd come out and* visit in my twenties, and through our many walks and talks. I feel I have become a better soul through our knowing each other!

I feel honored and blessed that you have let me into your life during this hard time. I don't know about you, but I feel a deeper love bond through this experience. Love transcends anything physical, and it is timeless. Thank you for you being you and living so authentically and teaching from your being.

I am going to end this letter with a couple of sentences that help me grow as soul and comfort me.

Divine Love is that essence which unites all reality and brings together all souls. If people look for love, they will find it.

I think the bottom line is that we have always looked for love in our relationship, and we have always found it!

With deep, Divine Love,
Marian

Rajita called me after she got this letter and said it made her cry because she could feel my love. One never knows when the last day will be for anyone; there is only now.

# Rajita's Turnabout

J EAN AND I WERE TRYING TO DIGEST RAJITA'S TURNABOUT
since previously she only allowed us to talk about healing and curing her cancer. She really didn't like us asking
about her pain. Now she talked freely about her pain level,
and about dying consciously. The three of us decided to
get together in the spring before Rajita became too weak
to enjoy our visit. No date was set because we left it up to
Rajita to let us know when she wanted us in Oregon.

A month earlier Rajita had called me, and we
recorded the conversation. I was the executrix of her estate
and had power of attorney—I would handle her bills,
make sure her wishes were carried out, and dispose of her
Earthly belongings. She really didn't have much in the
way of money or possessions, but there were things that
still had to be handled. This conversation was about the
business end of wrapping up her life, and it was an extremely emotionally draining conversation for me. Here

my sister was dealing with her death with complete responsibility and calmness. I knew if I let on how much sorrow I was feeling it would not help Rajita. Too much outward emotion from Jean or myself would, I felt, have undermined Rajita's focus and drained her strength.

So I listened, keeping my grief to myself, until after the phone call ended. Rajita told me when she wanted her website to be shut down, and we discussed other particulars of closing accounts and settling bills and making sure all was in order when she died. Her demeanor was calm and businesslike. The phone conversation left me drained and extremely sad. The reality of my sister dying soon was hitting me between my eyes. The thin veil of fantasy that she might survive was being ripped away.

What blew me away was how controlled she seemed. Intuitively, I sensed she would be distressed if she truly let herself feel all the emotions that must be under the surface.

*I will never know for sure what my sister was feeling, but my business for the last twenty-five years has been helping people confront hidden, subconscious emotions and beliefs. I am mostly spot-on in my estimate of what is really going on with someone, whether they are conscious of their issues or not.*

I never confronted or coaxed her into talking about her true feelings. I felt that would be counter-productive for my sister. So I listened and listened and listened some more, sending her love and dealing with my emotions through my support system of my husband, friends, and professionals.

I never cried, not even a little, when my mom died when I was twenty-one. That may sound cold, but I am really a deeply emotional person. When I was growing up I internalized the immeasurable pain I felt about her being sick my whole life and not ever being able to be a "mom" for me. The pain and true terror I felt at being on my own at fifteen was too overwhelming to allow myself to feel emotions consciously. So when my mom died when I was twenty-one, all I felt was numbness.

I have done an enormous amount of emotional healing since then. Now I feel comfortable in my skin. Emotions are something I can deal with in a healthy way, even though at times, like with my sister dying, it is extremely difficult. Experiencing my sister's journey with cancer, her attitude throughout every phase, and our closeness was a gift for me to heal more deeply my childhood loss, fears, and grief. As the weeks and short months went on, I had many more opportunities to do just that.

## RAJITA'S LAST WORKSHOP

Rajita, unbelievably, was still working, conducting webinars, and getting ready for her last workshop with her interns. Her workshop at the beginning of February would entail ten days away from her home and was several hours away by car. Conducting a workshop of this intensity and the travel it involved would be hard for a healthy person, much less someone in my sister's condition.

Rajita allowed herself to be helped and found someone to drive her to the seminar location. Throughout the ten days she would never be alone so Jean and I felt if anything happened she absolutely would get the help she needed. Rajita contacted us infrequently during her workshop, as she wanted to stay focused and the cell phone reception was spotty. I had to trust when I did not hear from her that she was OK.

The Mandala process Rajita invented was one of deep introspection. People took her course to help heal all kinds of issues in their lives including (of all things) cancer. I think the more profound purpose of her teaching this methodology was to help individuals see themselves as Soul, release attachments, and open their hearts to Divine Love. Rajita brought her extensive art training and talent into this process. Each person was given a sheet of paper that was black in color and an assortment of colored pencils. Rajita would then help workshop attendees to face the emotions and beliefs that were limiting them through the meditations and drawings they did.

Rajita was always experimenting and expanding her workshops. I believe as her cancer progressed she also started to integrate how to die into her teachings. She was getting on-the-job training, so to speak. During part of this last training her arrhythmia was very intense. One of her interns had to conduct several parts of the workshop she wanted to do herself. Rajita told us later that part of her thought it extremely ironic that the intern was teaching about death and dying because she was too sick to teach the class. Back in her room, she was experiencing another bout of arrhythmia while contemplating when her own death would come and what it would be like. Rajita came back to Ashland after her workshop very tired, but at peace that she had completed her purpose.

<hr/>

## ANOTHER VISIT TO OREGON

Jean and I were still wondering when Rajita wanted us to come out to Oregon. We wanted to go, but at the same time we knew that when we got that call it would mean her health was deteriorating even more. Jean and I were learning detachment in our own seminar of hard knocks.

Her call came about a week after she returned from her workshop. She wanted to be strong enough to be able to do things with us when we arrived. Jean and I thought we would be going in March or April, not February. Rajita's energy and health were failing quicker than we anticipated. We knew this was coming but we were both crushed. We all settled on February 24th. Jean and I would stay for about six days.

The mission of this trip was to help Rajita find a good hospice, meet her patient advocates who lived in Ashland, and spend some quality time with her. In my spiritual exercises every day I asked to be a vehicle of love and support for my sister and I asked for continued strength. As it turned out, I needed more than I could have ever imagined.

---

## MORE DEATH

Right around the time Rajita revealed she was seeking palliative care instead of focusing on curing her cancer, my wonderful, loving little office cat Bear started going blind and having strokes. Just six months earlier I had put down Zippity, who stopped eating after many years of strokes. Her little body had given out, and neither Mark nor I wanted her to suffer.

I sang HU softly to Zippity when she passed and then I felt this enormous wave of love flood over me when she left her body. I got over Zippity's passing more easily because of the enormity of the love I experienced when she died. Now six months later, Bear was having strokes and bumping into walls because she couldn't see.

By February Bear's blindness was complete. When she couldn't hear me she would give this pitiful, scared mew and she only calmed down when she'd heard my voice or smelled me near her. I could no longer let her outdoors and she so loved going outside. The little strokes were becoming more frequent. I was truly distraught. I loved Bear and wanted to do the right thing. I had learned through my experience with Zippity's sister Doo-Dah that I would not put an animal through painful procedures to give them—really me—more time.

Over the next couple of months I didn't know when my sister would need me to help her translate (pass) into death. I didn't want Bear to be scared and alone or die from a stroke by herself without me there. So I made the incredibly hard decision to put Bear down. I scheduled the vet to come to my office to do this a week before I was to go out to Oregon to help my sister.

I asked God for a waking dream: If this was for Bear's highest good, let me see some signs of her failing health within the next two weeks. Well, those next two weeks were filled with Bear crying out in fear when she didn't know I was there, and she had at least two other strokes. I felt pounded with grief.

Beth has been my best friend since I was married to my first husband. We have the same irreverent humor and slant on life. I can come to her about anything, she is there for me, and I can be real about my feelings. During this time Beth was a shoulder for me to cry on. Beth lost her father to a long battle with cancer, and I knew she understood the grief and crazy feelings that can arise. I told her about having to go and see my sister and what this trip meant. Then I told her about my decision to put down Bear before I left to help my sister. She paused and in her sweet North Dakota voice she said, "Marian, you are dealing with the pu pu platter of death over there." Through my tears I could not stop laughing. I knew in my heart of hearts she was not being flippant, but was helping me with humor, which I desperately needed. Laughter has always been my savior in hard times as well as good ones.

The fateful day arrived and I was still asking for more confirmation from Spirit that I was doing the best thing for Bear. The vet was coming to my office for this, but she was late. With every minute that passed I was becoming more engulfed with a lack of courage. When she arrived, before

I could say a word, she proceeded to tell me about a dog patient that died of a stroke just that morning. He could hear and had many little strokes over the last six months. His owners thought he was getting better. But, my vet informed me, these kinds of strokes are misleading. The animal seems to be getting better because animals learn how to self-correct their movements. They quickly learn how to walk and improvise from the effects of the strokes, but all the time their systems are really shutting down.

The dog's people found him dead on the floor that morning. He had died alone. This was my final confirmation. It was almost exactly what Bear had been going through. I did not want her to die alone and scared. I was with her singing HU and sending her love when she passed. I wish I could say I felt the same kind of love surge through me that I felt with Zippity, but I didn't. Grief, many times, blocks the receptors at the time of death to feeling the love of the Soul that is passing. Dealing with my sister, thinking about what I would have to face when I saw her, and losing yet another beloved kitty—I was utterly drained!

I spent the rest of that Saturday walking in the park and crying—crying for Bear, my sister, and myself.

CHAPTER

II

# Remembering a Prediction

EARLY IN JANUARY OF 2009, I HAD GIVEN A TALK TO A business group. I had arrived early and was killing time in my car, calling friends on my mobile phone. I reached my friend Lynda at home, and she immediately asked about my sister. I recounted for several minutes the courage, bravery, and spiritual determination my sister was conveying. "Rajita wants to live with spiritual consciousness of Divine Love and awareness through to the very moment of her passing," I said to Lynda.

Lynda had been privy to the incredible journey of my sister and me. Then she offhandedly said, "This should be a book." As soon as she said that, I remembered my dream from over twenty years ago that predicted I would write *two* books that would help elevate the consciousness of many people. I had written my first book, *You Are Soul*, many years ago. I never had an inspiration to write another book, until now.

Lynda's remark was God speaking to me through another. (That's when what is said hits you between the eyes, so to speak. This is what Lynda's remark did to me. It woke me to my mission.)

From that moment on I kept a journal of my dreams, spiritual occurrences, and the day-to-day interplay with Rajita and her journey. I have kept a dream journal for about twenty-five years, but I had not been writing down any details regarding Rajita until Lynda talked about my writing a book.

Besides dreams I wrote little letters to God in my journal asking for guidance and strength. In one of the letters after I talked to Lynda, I asked for unequivocal guidance about whether I was really supposed to write this book. I would go sleep singing HU, a prayer of Divine Love, sending love to my sister.

A month later I had a Soul Travel experience.

*Soul Travel is not astral projection, but the simplest way to describe it is the expansion of consciousness. Most people experience it as a sort of gradual shifting of awareness.*

All night I had the awareness of hearing and feeling this book being dictated to me. The best description is akin to information being downloaded into my brain. I could hear it, including the title, *Dancing with God . . . A True Story.*

I had my answer.

———◆◆◆———

## FEBRUARY 24:
## OUR TRIP TO SEE RAJITA BEGINS

Jean came from Florida the night before we left and stayed at my house overnight. That night Mark made us a wonderful fish chowder dinner. No one stayed up late as we had an early flight the next morning and Mark had a busy business day planned. My husband knew this trip was going to be extremely hard on me and since he had to work, he scheduled a car to take Jean and me to the airport. Atlanta traffic is horrendous and he wanted to make my trip a little easier, especially coming back home, knowing I would be feeling drained.

The car arrived for us at five-fifteen in the morning, and we touched down at the Medford Oregon airport at around noon Pacific Time. The plane trip was thankfully uneventful. During the flight Jean and I shared that we would like to be present for Rajita when she passed.

After Jean and I landed we took a cab straight to Rajita's apartment. She was extremely grateful for our coming, but Rajita looked weak and was not doing well

**Affirmations** Part of what I write in my dream journals, besides dreams and my letters to God, are affirmations to help me grow spiritually. The affirmations I choose have changed through the years, according to my needs and consciousness. During the last year of Rajita's life the affirmation I wrote almost exclusively was *Through all my actions and thoughts Divine Love flows.* Writing affirmations helps you create. The act of writing helps you connect to your subconscious mind and, depending what you write, can help you grow spiritually.

When writing affirmations, keep them in the present tense. The subconscious mind knows and operates only in the present. So if you write something like, "I will do such and such," it will stay always in the future.

I write affirmations either three times or fifteen times. Both numbers are quite powerful. I really don't know why, but affirmations do work more powerfully when you use these methods.

at all. Her heart had been in arrhythmia all day, beating furiously and erratically. New tumors were growing on her skull and neck. Even so, she wanted to participate in our arrival. I insisted that I drive her car to our hotel; Rajita agreed to let me. This was a huge concession for my sister. Once again, Rajita was extremely generous and had paid beforehand for a lovely hotel room for Jean and me to share. And once more she did this without our knowledge.

The hotel was cozy and lovely and within walking distance of her apartment and the center of town. Rajita had baskets with candy and wine waiting for us in our room, just like she did in Carmel. We left our bags and I drove us back to her place for a little meal of homemade soup. It was getting more and more difficult for Rajita to eat, so we planned to cook and eat our meals at her house. Sadly, going to restaurants together on our visit this time was out of the question.

We left early so she could rest. Jean and I needed exercise, so we walked around Ashland exploring what it had to offer. As I mentioned before, it is an adorable little town. We stopped for tea and coffee before heading back to our hotel. The beauty of our hotel's location was that we could get anywhere by walking. Both of us loved and needed those walks. We crashed early since we were still on East Coast time. Jean and I are compatible travelers and that made the trip a little easier. Our body clocks have the same rhythm. So we were in sync with the time of going to bed and getting up and when to eat.

## FEBRUARY 25: UNFINSHED BUSINESS

Today we needed to help Rajita with the unfinished business of finding a hospice, deciding what type of care she might need, and how she wanted her last days to be. Rajita's arrhythmia was slowly getting better. I was so glad

Jean was there with me. I don't think I would have been able to emotionally handle all that needed to be done without her presence and support. We talked about that, and Jean said she felt the same way.

Jean made lunch and cleaned while Rajita showed me how to handle her accounts and download money from them. I was recording the passwords and writing down what I needed to do when the time came that she could no longer take care of her finances. Then Rajita and I walked around her apartment, and I made a list of her personal effects and who would receive each item. I was numb. I kept saying to myself, "I have to be strong for my sister." If I felt even a hint of tears I shoved them back. My crying would not help Rajita nor help me at this juncture; there would be plenty of time for that later. We worked most of the morning and had lunch together. Then, exhausted, Rajita had to rest.

Jean and I went on another stroll around Ashland. During that walk I kept getting a nudge to check Rajita's bank, which was located on Main Street, to see if all was in order. I found out having the power of attorney meant I could write checks if she was unconscious, but that right stopped with her death. Not what I wanted to hear. We absolutely had to straighten that out before I left Oregon.

Rajita didn't want to get together for dinner because

she needed to rest, so Jean and I went back to our room and collapsed. Needless to say, we did indulge in the candy and wine. I called Mark and told him about the long, hard day. He listened and asked all the right questions. Next, I called my best friend Beth and told her everything. She mostly listened. Through both calls I felt supported and ready for the onslaught of the next day.

## FEBRUARY 26:
## MEETING THE MEDICAL ADVOCATES

Yesterday was long and very tough. After a quick breakfast, we got ready to meet Maureen and Gayle. Rajita had picked them as her local medical advocates. She had met them through other people at a breakfast meeting, and then they kept running into each other at different coffee houses in Ashland. My sister felt their positive energy, and after she got to know them better, she eventually asked them if they'd be her advocates locally. They readily agreed.

Rajita had invited them to her apartment for lunch so we could meet them. Jean made a killer chicken salad specifically for this meeting. From interacting with them at lunch both Jean and I knew they were perfect! They were totally on Rajita's side and they were the kind of people who could not be bullied by anyone. Maureen was familiar with the process of death, as she had helped her mother through a long illness and helped her pass. Gayle was just as strong, and they were good friends to boot.

Rajita wanted to make sure the doctors would not revive her if she lost consciousness. In her religion her body needed to be cremated within twenty-four hours of her passing. It was vitally important to Rajita that she had people she could trust to accomplish these things.

After lunch we talked with Maureen about her experiences with caring for her mother though her fight with cancer. Then the topic turned to Rajita's cremation and how she wanted her body prepared when she translated. Her body was to be washed after death as her spiritual practice dictated. Maureen said hospice could do that, but Gayle suggested, "Maybe you'd want someone close to you to do that."

Rajita then turned to me and asked, "Do you think you could wash and dress me after I die?"

Inwardly I was screaming, "Are you out of your mind?" Outwardly I said calmly, "I'll have to think about it." I could also sense Jean shouting in her head, "No freaking way." I avoided looking at Jean because I knew I'd break out into inappropriate laughter (which is one way I handle stress) at the bizarre request. (Now you may not think twice about bathing and dressing your dead sister, but I am just not built that way.)

Shortly after that unique conversation, Maureen and Gayle signed papers legally making them my sister's medical advocates if Jean and I were not present.

Both Jean and I felt incredibly relieved that Rajita had Maureen and Gayle to help her. Rajita was getting weaker each week, and we all knew her time for passing over would be soon. We were so far away and felt incredibly powerless much of the time.

When they left, Rajita, Jean, and I went to Rajita's bank to make me co-owner on her accounts. We wanted that cleared up as soon as possible. It was an easy thing to do, and if we didn't get it done by the time of her death, it would have created an enormous hairball of complications for me. Being on her accounts as co-owner meant I had complete ability at any time to write checks, even after her death. After we accomplished that, we went for a short walk in the park off Main Street. Rajita didn't have the energy to walk for long, but we were happy to share even a little stroll with her.

Our plan for the next day was to go to the crematorium and get that paperwork all squared away—something else to look forward to.

That day I observed the normal flow of life, people going about their day, and felt like I was in the Bermuda

Triangle. What was transpiring was so unbelievably intense for me. I felt isolated from normal life. I do think, though, these sorts of feelings are common when you are going through this kind of journey with someone you love.

That night Jean and I were so tired that we had to drag our little bodies to our hotel room. We were emotionally exhausted. I called Mark and Beth, my lifelines of normalcy. I recounted the do-you-want-to-wash-my-dead-body story. True to his witty self, Mark said, "It's just another one of those things I never thought I would hear anyone say." He and Beth worked their magic of logic, love, and wit to help me handle the enormity of this situation.

Jean and I went to sleep early and woke up as usual at five in the morning. She took a shower and got ready while I sang HU and did my spiritual contemplation. Both of us were ready for tea and coffee by seven sharp. We were like two kids with their noses pressed against the window waiting for the door to the breakfast room to open. When it did, look out! I needed caffeine and food and we wanted to nab our now-favorite table by the window overlooking a beautiful garden. This quiet and serene setting gave us a little respite of peace and solace, which we sorely needed.

We called my sister to see if she was up. To our great surprise she was already at the park! Well, we scampered our little rear-ends out the door and met Rajita for a really good walk. She showed us more of the park, like the really cool places where all the ducks hung out. We walked for a good hour. Then it was off to the crematorium—yet another reminder of the things to come.

Rajita had already researched the local crematoriums. Very much a person in control of her life, she picked a place that was affordable and agreed to have her body cremated within twenty-four hours of her death. We met the owner, who seemed kind and caring.

Rajita, of course, was not feeling well and she came across as edgy and a little angry. This was understandable under the circumstances. I personally think going to the actual physical location of a funeral home was bringing up a fear of death she did not want to acknowledge, at least to us. I know from my own growth and my work helping others that anger can mask fear. I don't know how I would handle what Rajita went through, but I personally wished she could have let herself be held and cry her heart out. But this was not about what I wanted or needed; it was about my sister and how she wanted to approach her life and her death.

After that was done we went to her apartment for a short visit. Jean and I were leaving early the next morning. All the pieces were in place now to protect and care for

Rajita. Jean and I could leave feeling relieved, but our hearts were definitely filled with sorrow.

Our intention, which we shared with Rajita, was to be in close contact with hospice as time went on. Hospice workers have a pretty good idea when someone is close to passing. When they thought the end was near, they would notify us and we would come out to be with her when she died and take care of her place afterward. That was the plan, and Rajita was in complete agreement. Later that day, Rajita dropped us off at our hotel. Before she got into her car we hugged her goodbye. We told her we loved her and that if it were meant to be, we would be at her side, holding her hands at the time of her passing, just like we planned. She never cried, not even once.

We went back to our room and discussed her lack of emotional connection. To this day I believe that if she had let herself feel too much she could not have emotionally dealt with her impending death.

## CHAPTER

## 12

# Coming to Terms

## MARCH 5: CRYING

I HAD BEEN HOME NOW FOR FIVE DAYS, SEEING CLIENTS AND catching up on my life. The night before, I cried for the first time since I got back from my trip. And I cried a lot. I had just gotten off the phone with Rajita. She was in arrhythmia again and to my amazement she was crying! This was the first time she had cried with me. I believed she felt she would die soon. I was just so exhausted. She reiterated that she wanted Jean and me to be there when she passed.

## MARCH 6: A CALL FROM RAJITA

I was crocheting a comforter and watching TV with Mark when Rajita called. She said more and more people from her past were connecting with her—people she had not heard from in years, some for more than twenty years.

None of them knew directly that she was dying, they just got the nudge to contact her. One example of this was when she conducted a talk near Ashland in January and her ex-husband showed up. Rajita had been divorced for about thirty years and the last time she had seen her ex-husband was about twenty years ago. After her talk that night they exchanged pleasantries. She did not tell him about her cancer. Rajita did confide in both Jean and me later that hearing from all these people (including seeing her ex-husband) was a sign of closure for her.

During our conversation she also admitted she had just enough energy to talk to either Jean or me every day, but not both. This meant Jean and I would take turns calling Rajita, and then one would phone the other and tell what was happening.

Ever practical, Rajita discussed what kind of container she wanted for her ashes. She didn't want to spend a lot of money and she suggested we could use a Tupperware container. "After all," she said, "I won't be here." Yeah, but I will, I thought. I told her firmly and (hopefully) respectfully that I could not disrespect her by putting her ashes in a plastic food container. Just the thought of that creeped me out. After this conversation I felt completely drained. Part of me, I knew, was trying to handle the myriad emotions that were surfacing.

When I get overwhelmed I get tired and want to sleep and this is exactly how I felt.

———◆———

## MARCH 18: ARRHYTHMIA AGAIN

Rajita was in arrhythmia again. Fourth time this month. In her spiritual practice there are certain chants people do for helping Soul pass at death. She was looking into recording them so she could play them on her MP3 in case no one could be there in person to chant for her. I believed she believed her death would be very soon. I did, too. I also knew I was healing old grief from my childhood as well as the present grief of Rajita dying.

That night I was thinking I might never see Rajita alive again, and she might not live to see her birthday on May 8th. So I decided to send her a birthday gift a month and half early, a poem I wrote from my heart that night. I couldn't think of anything else that made sense so I sent her my love through the auspices of the poem.

My birthday gift to you, Rajita!

I will never forget you.

When I see the hummingbirds

on the flowers

I will know you are saying "hi."

When a stray kitten comes to me for a pat

I will be thinking of you

and open my heart

to an inner communication

of Love, Joy, and Soul.

Know you will not be forgotten.

Love transcends the physical body

and links Soul to Soul!

I put that poem in a birthday card the next day and sent it to my sister. When Rajita received it she told me it made her weep, and she thanked me and said she would treasure it.

---

## MARCH 28: CELEBRATING MY BIRTHDAY

My birthday was the 25th, and I experienced a multitude of emotions I did not expect. Saying it was hard for me to be happy and celebrate my birthday while my sister was in pain and dying is elementary. What I didn't expect were the waves of experience these feelings had on me when they poked their little heads up and said, "Hi."

My husband took me to Starbucks for afternoon tea on my birthday. We love going there, and it is always a treat (after all, we are yuppies at heart). Right in the middle of drinking my chai latte I burst into tears. Spontaneously combusting into a sobbing mess took me completely by surprise.

All day long my friends were calling and emailing me "Happy Birthday" wishes. I felt so much love. Love is always uplifting. The love I was receiving was helping me to heal, and my tears were helping me to cope.

On some level I knew this, and yet all I could think about was Rajita. That she was getting so weak she could no longer clean her own house, that her tumors were growing, and she could only see visitors for about an hour at a time because she was so sick.

———»•«———

## APRIL 2: DREAMING OF DEATH

I dreamed Rajita died. I was crying all during the dream. In the dream I was confused about whether I was dreaming or not. The dream was able to convey to me that Rajita's energy was blocked about dying. Someone (it felt like a spiritual guide) told my sister, "Just go, just focus on the wings, not on the physical." And she did. While I heard the voice I saw these huge, beautiful blue wings in the sky. Telepathically they were directing my sister to go toward the blue wings of Light.

In the dream I telephoned Jean. I was crying, but she was doing fairly well. I said, "Rajita died and needs to be cremated right away." My dream faded away with me vaguely aware of seeing my dead brother Robert.

———»•«———

## APRIL 5: WHAT THE DREAM MEANT

When I first had that dream I really didn't give it a lot of thought, and I almost discounted what it was trying to convey. The true deeper meaning of the dream was revealed to me after I talked with Rajita.

In our conversation, Rajita revealed she was in much greater pain than she had let on. She told me she did not want a long, lingering, debilitating death like our parents had. If Jean and I were fortunate enough to be at her side while she was dying, she asked us not to engage her in idle talk. She wanted to concentrate on the process and make it as conscious and spiritual as possible. We could hold her hands but not talk. I told her I would inform Jean of her request, and we would honor it. (I would find out later that this was easier said than done.)

After our discussion I went for a run at this beautiful green beltway by my office. It was built as a path for bikes and running and had trails in the woods for mountain bikes and non-bikers. It was a safe place, and one could travel the trails for miles and miles.

I often get inspiration and insights when I run, and that day was no exception. I thought of my conversation with Rajita all the time I ran. The true meaning and, more importantly, the emotional acceptance of the dream hit me like a ton of bricks.

Rajita had the choice of when to pass from her body, but her attachment to the physical love of the people around her was keeping her here. I had promised her in our phone conversation to not engage her at the end, and I realized this could be the end, right now, if she wanted it to be. Inwardly, as I jogged, I gave her my wholehearted agreement and permission (really my non-attachment to her physical presence) to go on.

While I ran I sobbed. I felt the full impact of what I realized on every level of my being. I let myself cry, but like always I tried to do it as a way of healing so I could be stronger. I have experienced personally and with my clients that repressing feelings leads to unconscious negative results, physically and/or emotionally.

My sobbing was my way of detaching and helping my sister. During my jog I asked God, "Should I let my sister know the whole truth about my dream and the realization I gleaned from it?" I asked for an immediate sign, something out of the ordinary. If I should tell my sister, I requested, let me see something blue that is not usually blue and I needed to have this sign shown to me before I went home from my run. When I came out of the trail in the wooded area, I immediately saw a blue construction barrel in the parking lot. (In Georgia they are usually orange, not blue.) This one was blue and right in front of me as I emerged from the woods. Never in my life had I ever seen a blue construction barrel!

*I personally do not believe anyone should reveal spiritual information you get in contemplations or dreams unless you*

*have gotten the spiritual guidance to do so. This is why I
asked for such a definitive sign and within a specific time
frame. I never want to trespass into another's spiritual space
or violate any boundary of another person.*

That night I emailed Rajita and informed her about
the dream. I told her that the dream revealed that she had
the spiritual grace to leave this planet now, if she would
face her fears of death and release her emotional attachments to leaving her loved ones. She never commented
on the email, which I thought was telling. Over the years
she asked numerous times about my dreams and if any
were pertinent to her.

## APRIL 10: MORE LETTING GO

Found out today Rajita was giving her car away. She was
no longer able to drive, yet another reminder that her energy was failing fast.

## APRIL 27: ANOTHER DREAM

I had another vivid dream. Rajita and I were talking Soul
to Soul. We were both glowing light. Rajita was worried
about me, and how I would handle her passing. I told her

I could handle it and not to worry. Then the dream faded.

## APRIL 29: FASTING

Over the last two weeks Rajita had been discussing her desire to fast. At the end of a long illness the body naturally shuts down. You stop eating and eventually stop drinking, and the body dies. Animals do this instinctively.

In Rajita's religion she had to get permission to do this consciously, as opposed to it happening out of her control. No matter what *your* individual beliefs may be about fasting at a time like this, *she* was handling it with the utmost sacred care. Rajita did not want to incur any negative karma, which you can do if you are not willing to confront what you came here to face by ending your life prematurely. Though her life was coming to an end, I believe her overriding desire was to leave her body consciously with spiritual grace and awareness and not incur any negative karma.

I will admit I grappled with the idea of her fasting and all the ramifications it meant for me with my beliefs. I do believe there are individuals with higher states of consciousness who pick the day they will leave their bodies and they just go—as Soul they just leave their bodies. They don't shoot or poison themselves. They have earned the grace to have the ability to leave their bodies at will when their mission and purpose is done here on Earth.

———◆◆◆———

## MAY 2: PERMISSION TO FAST

Rajita got permission from her spiritual leaders to fast. She sounded peaceful about her decision and said she would probably start May 4. She had to get health care people in place first before she started the fast. In her condition, once she started fasting she could become unconscious very quickly.

I called hospice and talked to Rajita's nurse. I asked her how long it takes for someone in my sister's condition to pass when they fast. Jean's and my intentions still stood. We wanted to be present for Rajita when she died, but neither of us has unlimited resources of money or the emotional energy it would take to be physically present watching a loved one die for weeks while away from our own families. It would be difficult enough if Rajita were in the same city, but her being three thousand miles away created a whole other level of hardship.

The nurse said that, to the best of her knowledge, if my sister, being as thin as she was, stopped drinking as well as eating it would be much faster, as little a few days to a week or so. If Rajita decided to continue drinking she could last as long as a month. No one knew for sure.

Rajita was now letting us both talk to her each day. The phone calls were flying between Jean and me. We were trying to comprehend all that was taking place. My digestion was a mess due to the massive stress I was under.

## MAY 3: A PARTING VISUALIZATION

To the people closest to her, Rajita sent a transcript via email of what she would like everyone to visualize for her when it came time for her to leave her body. I chose to ask for her highest good instead of visualizing. (When I do this or anyone else asks something from that consciousness, the request is in the hands of God. You may not get what you want from an ego standpoint, but you will always get the next step for your growth as Soul.) I never told Rajita I was not visualizing for her the way she wanted, just that I was supporting her and I would see her surrounded in Divine Love.

Jean and I were getting very jumpy, and my golf game was sucking wind. Rajita was contacting people she trusted to set up a team to help her through her physical needs and spiritual needs, even when she became unconscious. I was increasingly amazed at the depth of detail and planning Rajita was giving to her own death. How many people, given the same circumstances, would choose to leave this planet as consciously as possible?

━━►◆◄━━

## MAY 4: STARTING THE FAST

I found out Rajita was starting her fast on her birthday, which is May 8th. Earlier she told us she was going to start a few days before her birthday. Rajita had told Jean to get the plane tickets for her and me so we could be there on the 10th. At the time Jean purchased the tickets Rajita would have been fasting for a solid week, and very close to passing. This was our original joint plan. Now when we got there she would have been fasting for only, at most, two days and she could linger for weeks. Every time Jean and I talked to her she was moving the day of her fast. This sounds awful, but I felt manipulated by my sister. I was trying to grapple with being authentic to myself and being supportive of her. Guilt, for me, is no reason to do anything. In my sessions I teach my clients that guilt is self-punishment and stops the flow of love. You can learn anything in this life with love instead of guilt. Now I was being tested greatly.

I wanted to support my sister, but I absolutely did not want to lose myself in the process.

This inwardly reminded me of how my mother treated

177

me when she was sick. My mom would manipulate me, whether consciously or not, for her own emotional needs. I was too young when that was happening to help myself, but now I could. I still felt conflicted, and anger was starting to surface. I kept my anger mostly to myself but discussed my feelings with Mark and Beth. In this circumstance, even though I am a therapist, I still found it hard not to put myself down for the anger I was feeling. Deep down I knew there was a very good reason for my feelings. I view all feelings as teachers. They are teaching you something; you just have to find out what.

<hr>

## MAY 5: DEALING WITH RAW EMOTIONS

Jean talked to Rajita early in the morning. Then Jean called me when I was at my office. Luckily I was between clients. Jean informed me Rajita was starting her fast now a day later. I completely lost it! I was alone in my office and with all the stress, grief, and worry about how I could juggle being away, I blew up. Now that must sound awfully cold, but my heart was broken. Because of the information I gleaned from the hospice nurse, I learned it was more than likely that I would not be physically present for my sister's passing. I also intuitively knew Rajita wanted us with her as long as possible because she was afraid.

On the phone Jean stayed calm in spite of my meltdown, which consisted of sobbing and yelling at the same time. Something was off with this agenda of Rajita's, I just knew it. But I couldn't put it into words or realize what it meant until later. I was certain, though, I could not have an open-ended ticket and stay in Ashland watching her die for weeks. I just didn't have it in me.

After I hung up from my call with Jean, I called Beth and Mark. Through my conversations with them, they separately conveyed the same advice. They both felt Rajita was being manipulative, whether she was aware of it or not. (Also dying doesn't make manipulation right or good for anyone.)

Both suggested I get clear about what was right for my life at this juncture. When you understand what your boundaries are, no one can manipulate you. With that clarity, I could go help Rajita with an intention of service and not come from guilt or anger. Knowing my boundaries was absolutely imperative for me at this juncture. This was great advice, which I took to heart.

After I assimilated their advice I did calm down and felt more at peace. Inwardly I got clear, crystal clear, as to what was right for me. I knew I had to have a conversation with Rajita and tell her how long I was going to stay. This exchange was not going to be easy. The tickets Jean bought were for a nine-day trip. We would arrive on May 10th and leave on May 18th.

My decision to let Rajita know my plans and that I would be leaving on the ticketed day of departure was firmly in place in my mind. By this time Rajita had changed the day she was to start fasting at least four or five times. I really didn't know if she'd even go through with the fast. She could also decide not to fast at any time. I could not keep my life on hold, live at this stress level, and keep a business and a marriage intact. I comprehended totally what I needed to do for my health and well-being.

I went running to burn off excess anger. After my run I found a quiet spot and did a short but meaningful contemplation, ending it with singing the HU. When someone is controlling or manipulative, reaction to another's boundaries is usually met with anger or more manipulation. I was steeling myself for just such a reaction. I was not disappointed.

I called Rajita right there on the trail after my contemplation. Rajita picked up right away, and the first words out of her mouth were filled with her own anxieties of not finding a caregiver to help her with the medications and her physical needs during the fast. Staying focused, calm and logical, I asked her how many people she interviewed and she replied, "Two." She emphasized she couldn't find a caregiver in the small town. Rajita sounded on the verge of hysteria. This was one of the few times I heard fear in her voice. I rationally reaffirmed she would find someone, and said the hospice nurse would have leads for people in that field.

Then the conversation went from bad to worse. She asked if I would do the medications for her if she could not find anyone. This meant rectal applications because she would be fasting. I kept my voice steady, yet I tried to convey kindness and love while saying that I would not do this. I reaffirmed I would help in other ways with washing her hair and trips to the bathroom, but I was not comfortable giving these kinds of medications.

She then accused me of abandoning her and not being there for her. That hurt me to my very core. I knew it was not true, yet I was so raw at this time that her saying this deeply wounded me. After that she hung up on me, saying she couldn't talk to me right then.

Dazed from the onslaught of our conversation, I went home and Mark asked how it went. He knew I'd be talking to my sister that afternoon. I looked at him and said, "It couldn't have gone any worse." He sat with me and let me cry and talk out loud about the last couple of days and all the swirling feelings I was going through. During that conversation I had a realization that was so clear it felt like a fog had lifted from inside of me. It was a true epiphany and healing all at the same time. What I was going through with my sister was what I had gone through with my mother. Now when I communicated a hard boundary with Rajita, a mother figure, I was healing the remainder of what I had lost of my authentic self, when my mother, unconsciously, had made me responsible for her happiness.

I woke up the next day with the realization I had to communicate, through email, our original plan. Originally, Jean and I told Rajita that we would stay in close contact with hospice and fly out when she was a couple of days away from passing. Rajita had been on board with that plan from its inception.

I wrote a clear, calm email recounting to Rajita our former intentions, reaffirmed that I loved her, and said I would do all that I could for her while I was there. I told her I would leave on the 18th, and said the time frame had gotten messed up because of the timing of her fasting and Jean's buying the tickets. I did not shame Rajita or express anger, I just explained the facts and conveyed over and over my love and support. It may not have been what she wanted, but under the circumstances it was all I could do.

I read it to Mark and Jean before I emailed it to Rajita. I wanted the tone of the email to be one of truth and support. Both Jean and Mark thought I communicated my

**Boundaries** You can never have a healthy relationship with yourself or another person without having healthy boundaries. Your boundaries are unique because you are a unique individual. Just because someone else may believe yelling, for example, is acceptable behavior, that does not mean you have to accept it. Maintaining your boundaries is the only action that creates health. If you state a boundary that is important to you to someone and don't follow through, you abandon yourself. With every boundary you define you teach people how to respect you. When you defend your own boundaries you build your self-respect and enhance your self-care.

When someone you know is dying, it is easy to lose perspective on what is really necessary for your health and well-being. It is another kind of dance. Your boundaries can change as you change. The key is to be truly honest with yourself about whether a particular boundary is important and necessary for you at any given time. Only you can answer this.

support and boundaries with the right tone.

At this time I had not heard anything from Rajita—no phone call or email. The next morning Jean called me from her cell phone. She and her husband were in the car somewhere in Virginia, driving from Florida to their summer home on the Saint Lawrence Seaway. This time it was Jean's turn to lose it. Rajita had called her and said my email was cold, and that I was abandoning and not supporting her. Before she knew it, Jean started screaming at the top of her lungs at Rajita. Anyone who knows Jean knows she is tolerant and kind. I'm much more likely to lose patience and get angry than Jean. So for her to start yelling at Rajita was very unusual.

Jean stuck up for me big time. She told Rajita she would not hear nor accept what she was saying because for all these years and now, Marian had been there for her. Jean told her in no uncertain terms she would not accept Rajita's negative behavior regarding me. Well, Jean's yelling shocked Rajita out of her behavior. She started to capitulate and see that, yes, indeed, she was loved and supported by both Jean and me.

Later that night I got a very short email from Rajita saying whenever I left Oregon would be fine with her and that she did love me. I do believe the cancer was affecting her thinking and her emotions. Regardless, I still had to do what was healthy for me, no matter how hard.

This occurrence in my life was such a dramatic experience of Divine Love. Keep in mind, love is always uplifting. If you knowingly let someone do you harm by allowing them to manipulate you, you have degraded your life and theirs. Keeping healthy boundaries is not always easy, but it is always uplifting.

CHAPTER

---

13

# Rajita's Last Days

## MAY 8: RAJITA'S BIRTHDAY!

MANY PEOPLE IN ASHLAND GATHERED TO ATTEND A birthday party celebration for Rajita near the big duck pond in the center of the park, which was her favorite place in that park. They brought food, cake, and love and admiration for her. She officially started her fast at two-fifteen that day.

The night before her birthday I had dreamed Rajita was at a gathering. In the dream I was told it was a pre-wake. She looked healthy and glowing white and I hugged her. She told us to enjoy ourselves and she was smiling. I got the sense I would be physically present when she passed.

Later that day my brother Michael and nephew Max flew to Oregon from California to see Rajita. This was Michael's birthday present to her, a surprise visit. She only had energy to talk to them for about an hour. Later Ulla, Rajita's caregiver, revealed to me that Rajita was very touched by Michael's surprise visit. I remembered from earlier conversations with Rajita that she so wanted to connect with him before she died.

On Rajita's birthday I played in a golf tournament. It was for a friend's birthday, and the rules were more goofy golf than real golf—all good fun, but I felt like I was playing through thick molasses. I couldn't hit a golf ball to save my life. All the while I was golfing I kept thinking, so much life going on while my sister is dying.

---

## MAY 10: TRAVELING TO OREGON

Jean and I planned to meet at the Atlanta airport and fly to Oregon together. As I was packing and getting ready to leave, my watch stopped working. I had had this watch for eight years, and it had never been slow or quit working . . . ever. I took this as a waking dream—a sign— that Rajita was getting very close to death.

Since our blowup over the phone Rajita had not really had a conversation with either Jean or me. She was in arrhythmia and weak. When either of us called her she couldn't talk to us because she said she was too tired. I also believed emotionally it was difficult for her to communicate honestly with me. That hurt, but my agenda was to help her cross. This was not about me, but about her needs at that juncture. The more I kept that in mind the better I could cope and help her.

When I met Jean at the airport the weather was bleak. I got to the airport almost four hours before our flight so I could get us seats together. For that particular flight, the airline withheld seating assignments until you arrived at the airport. I think the flight was overbooked and this was a way of weeding out stragglers. Right away I found this wonderful airline rep to help me find seats so Jean and I could sit together. I didn't even have to wait in line. I do believe she saw the grief plainly on my face. When I explained the situation, she was immediately helpful.

Jean flew in from Syracuse and when her plane landed in Atlanta we only had to wait an hour until we took off for Oregon. We arrived very late, around eleven that night, West Coast time. Already Jean and I were bone tired. Maureen and Gayle met us at the airport. It was so wonderful to see their friendly faces and feel their support. After we hugged they told us Rajita was not doing well, that she was in pain. Just another reminder of what we would encounter in the days ahead.

It was a short drive from the airport to our hotel. Once more, Rajita had booked and paid for our room at the same little hotel where we stayed on our last visit. We didn't know Rajita had paid for the room until we got there and checked in. And again we were surprised, since we never came with that expectation.

Part of Rajita's plan was to have several of her interns come and do the chanting to help her cross in death. They were staying with Rajita's good friend who had a big house in the center of town. Her generous friend offered to put up all the people coming to visit Rajita, even us. Before we arrived Jean and I had mutually decided we needed space away from other people, a place that would be a respite where we could go to recharge. Being around strangers at this time, twenty-four hours a day, would have been even more draining for us and we needed all the strength we could muster.

When we got to the hotel, we went right to bed. Neither Jean nor I wanted to wake Rajita at this late hour and we wanted to get as much sleep as possible because we had nine difficult days ahead.

---

## MAY 11: MEETING ULLA

At four sharp, Jean and I awoke and we were at Rajita's by seven-thirty that morning. Ulla, Rajita's caregiver, met us at the door. We liked Ulla right away; she emanated joy, life, and strength. Just what Jean and I were hoping Rajita's caretaker would be like.

I think many times in life people have an idea of how things "should" be and if reality does not match the vision in their minds it often leads to disappointment. The lesson for me in those situations, when I have a fixed idea of how something should be, is letting go of the attachment, seeing the lesson and learning from the situation as it is, not how I'd like it to be. This trip for me was a graduate program of learning this.

When we arrived at the apartment, Ulla took us right up to Rajita's bedroom so we could say hello. Immediately we knew she was experiencing a very bad attack of arrhythmia. Her heart was beating so fast we saw her pulse throbbing in her neck, even as we stood in the doorway of her bedroom. Her heartbeat was so rapid and strong that it looked like the vein in her neck would explode any minute. What was unbelievably devastating for us was that Rajita didn't want to see, talk, or spend time with us. She basically shushed us away after we said hello. That shocked us to our core.

Jean and I truly wanted to be there for Rajita at the time of her passing. In our minds this meant "loving on her," which is a Southern expression for giving physical and emotional affection. We visualized holding her hand and feeling Rajita's love returned. In our picture we were serving, but expecting something back. Instead we had just entered a boot camp of selfless service that we didn't even know we signed up for . . . consciously. Selfless serving is just that, no expectations of getting anything back, just giving out of love. This is not always easy, to say the least. In this circumstance both of us found it incredibly difficult.

Rajita's refusing to connect emotionally was not unusual, as we came to find out. Ulla told us this happens because the person who is dying wants to go inward, which is part of the process of dying. At that time I forgot what Rajita asked of us weeks ago—to not "engage" with her at the end so she could pass. I just saw my sister dying and experienced her not wanting to talk to me. Emotionally Jean and I were devastated and bewildered by Rajita's behavior.

We stayed at her apartment for about an hour talking to Ulla. In a very kind way, Ulla also shared with us that Rajita had been short tempered, critical, and controlling. Jean and I had already experienced this so we were not surprised by what Ulla revealed to us. We all felt that Rajita's anger and need for control were surfacing as part of her fear of death. No one was judging Rajita, just trying to honestly deal with an astonishingly difficult situation and help her the best we could.

After our conversation with Ulla, Jean and I left and went to the health food store to get some food and talk about the rest of our trip. I had a firm conviction and clarity to leave on the 18th, the day of our scheduled return flight. Jean was still undecided if she would stay however long it would take for Rajita to pass. I conveyed my opinion about not doing anything from guilt. Though I think guilt is destructive, I was not attached to trying to convince Jean either way. I would be supportive of whatever she decided. I just knew I could not emotionally endure a lengthy stay. What felt healthy for me was to stay for the amount of time we initially planned. I truly was at peace with my decision. No one had to understand or agree with it because it was my boundary, not anyone else's.

After seeing Rajita and experiencing her non-communication and lack of affection, Jean eventually came to the same decision. We both would leave on the 18th. Jean and I discussed at length about reframing our idea of this trip, from one of the ideal of Rajita and us exchanging goodbyes with warmth and affection, to one of selfless service. Jean and I realized we would not be getting any "warm fuzzies" from Rajita. We recommitted to help her pass from this life with as much love and care as we could give, regardless of what, if anything, we got back.

Later that day we went back to her place and again she did not want to talk to us. We then spoke with Ulla some more, went to dinner and back to our room. We were bushed and wanted a good night's sleep. Tomorrow we would start clearing out Rajita's Earthly belongings from the apartment.

━━━►•◄━━━

## MAY 12: SPIRITUAL HEALING

We got up at our usual four-thirty in the morning and waited impatiently for the breakfast nook to open so we could get our coffee and tea. I had stopped drinking coffee for over a year by then. Though I still missed the Starbucks runs my husband and I used to do each morning, I felt physically better for giving up coffee for tea.

Around seven we walked to Rajita's apartment. It was always a pleasant walk to her apartment as the air was crisp and the flowers were blooming in force. Rajita's little main room was now filled with plant life. Every surface held an assortment of lovely plants or colorful flowers. So many people had sent Rajita exquisite blooms for her birthday. I was so glad to see that and it truly warmed my heart to see how people loved her.

Ulla, though, was in tears when we arrived. This took us by surprise because though we had known Ulla for only a short time she appeared to be capable, strong, and not easily intimidated. By then she had been at my sister's place for more than thirty-six hours non-stop. She slept and ate there, which was part of a caregiver's job, but Rajita was becoming more critical and demanding, and this was becoming too much for Ulla. She told us that if she didn't get some help soon she might not be able to work with Rajita, and we would have to find a new caregiver. Well, Jean and I panicked. We absolutely did not want to lose Ulla. She was joyful and caring and competent, just what we wanted for our sister. We'd have a hard time replacing Ulla, as that combination is not easy to come by.

We told Ulla not to accept unkind behavior from my sister, even now. Jean and I recounted the story of our previous week—the phone calls and our anger and how Rajita accused me of abandoning her. This helped Ulla feel better, as she understood it was not about her. Being able to talk to us so honestly and having us validate her right to have her boundaries, even when someone was dying, helped Ulla heal old wounds of her own.

She confided in us that in the past when people in her life behaved badly, she would end up feeling bad or not good enough and then would forfeit her boundaries. Rajita's behavior was pushing her not-good-enough button now. Part of what Ulla was learning now, she confided, was to recognize and communicate her boundaries and confirm her own worth, regardless of anyone else's validation.

Ulla, Jean, and I were able to be completely honest about our feelings. For Jean and me this provided the emotional support we needed, even amongst strangers. Ulla was healing also, by sharing her feelings and having us listen to her and corroborate what she was going through. What profound gifts of personal growth we were all being given through such a hard life situation!

This reaffirmed for me that unfathomable healing and spiritual learning were taking place in so many dimensions for all the participants in Rajita's death. And the learning kept on coming. Jean and I encouraged Ulla to stay, and we called the hospice nurse and told her we needed a night person to ease the burden on Ulla. A meeting was set for the next day so we could put our heads together and find an assistant for Ulla. We were absolutely determined not to lose Ulla.

After the heartfelt exchange among the three of us, Ulla seemed confident we'd find her help. We tried in vain to connect with Rajita that day, but she continued to avoid talking with us. Together, Jean and I held her hand for a short time and silently gave her love. I sang HU inwardly and told her I loved her.

After that we got to work methodically clearing her apartment. This was what she wanted and had instructed us to do. Jean and I started packing dishes, clothes, and other household stuff. We accomplished a lot that day, but Jean and I called it quits after a few hours.

Amazingly, Rajita was taking very small doses of pain medications, considering her condition. The caregivers would ask her throughout the day and night if she wanted any pain meds, but she kept refusing them. All the food had been taken out of her place before her birthday at her request so she would not feel any temptation to eat.

Her interns were coming the next day. Rajita's plan was for them to chant the Hindu chant to help Soul cross over at eleven in the morning and four in the afternoon every day, until either she died or they had to go back to their respective homes. Rajita also had said she wanted to meditate every day and keep the chant going on her iPod speakers so she could hear it constantly. Ulla confided that Rajita stopped meditating and did not want to listen to her iPod. We all believed this was another sign of her going inward.

## MAY 13: TAKING CARE OF BUSINESS

Jean and I had our usual morning routine, coffee and tea at the hotel by the corner window overlooking the garden, our small respite in a hurricane-like onslaught of feelings. We then did the short ten-minute hike to Rajita's, talked with Ulla for a few minutes, and said hello to an unresponsive Rajita.

We were having our big meeting in the afternoon with the hospice nurse to find an all-night caregiver for Rajita. In the meantime, Jean and I got to work on closing Rajita's credit card accounts and other accounts that could be closed now, and paying bills. At eleven the women came to chant. They did the chanting in the other bedroom next to Rajita's. The chanting went on for about twenty minutes for each session. Every chant, just like every song, has its own vibration. Personally, Jean and I found this chant depressing. We were glad Rajita had the energy she wanted to help her cross, but it was one more thing we had to contend with that drained our energy. I am sure other people might have found the chant beautiful. Unfortunately, we did not, but it was our time to give and be tolerant.

Later that afternoon the hospice nurse came and the four of us brainstormed to get help for Ulla. The person we hired had to be right for Rajita. Jean and I worried that Ashland, being a small town, would be limited in the number of caregivers. Ulla had called every caregiver she knew the day before, with no success. After about an hour of discussion back and forth, I thought to ask the nurse about agencies. The light bulb went on and she immediately thought of two good ones. We called them right away and found the perfect person within an hour. Sherry would start the very next night. In addition to Sherry being a competent and kind caregiver, she had helped several yogis with their deaths, so we felt she would innately respect my sister and her beliefs.

This took a huge load off Jean and me. We knew our sister would be cared for and Ulla would stay. We needed Ulla almost as much as Rajita did. Jean and I appreciated our daily talks and Ulla's irreverent sense of humor. Someone else who might have been more serious would have been fine for my sister's physical needs, but Jean and I would have missed the daily relief we got from connecting with someone who really got us.

The interns, we found out, were all women and they were lovely, open, and friendly people. Jean and I met them all, and they dubbed us "the sisters." They practiced many different faiths, but what they had in common was their love and respect for Rajita, and in addition to their other wonderful traits they all had big, loving hearts.

One intern Jean and I liked immediately was Rosie, who also had an irreverent sense of humor and laughed easily. One of the first things I asked her was if she, too, practiced Hinduism like Rajita. She said, "You might say I am more of a HinJew and a BuJew." I nearly fell on the floor I laughed so hard. Both Jean and I felt it so necessary to laugh during this time. Being around others who didn't judge laughter around death and dying was truly a God-send to both of us.

Some information we gleaned from the interns was that Rajita wanted to leave her body consciously with spiritual grace and consciousness. A sign of that in Rajita's spiritual practice would be a rainbow near her body. Jean and I found out the interns that were here came from all over the States. As wonderful as they were, and they were phenomenal, it was difficult beyond words for Jean and me to witness our sister dying among strangers with no family there except each other. But that was how Rajita wanted it.

The weather that May was wonderful in Oregon, so Jean and I picked restaurants where we could eat outside. We had our big meal in the afternoons and nibbled at night. Jean and I were staying as busy as we could, so we took long walks every day after lunch to clear our minds as well as to get some exercise. Each day we made substantial headway with Rajita's belongings, and the apartment was looking pretty bare. We got rides when we needed to cart bigger things to our hotel room or when Jean and I had to go to UPS to ship items or to shred large piles of documents.

I located, with Maureen's help, someone who would come in after Rajita died and take the few remaining pieces of furniture to a shelter or to people who needed them. This assured me everything would be in order when I left.

---

## MAY 14: SEEING A RAINBOW

Rajita was extremely thin but she was still drinking a lot of water, which meant she could live for weeks. Jean and I would be long gone and, if it took longer than two weeks for Rajita to pass, we would have to find a replacement for Ulla. She signed up to work for only ten days because she had a vacation already planned. Every day Jean and I would go in and see Rajita and together hold her hand and talk to her. Now she had stopped talking to us totally. Rajita would talk to the caregivers to let them know if she needed meds and to answer their questions about bathing and such, but to our continual disappointment, she didn't communicate and share her thoughts with us. The seven interns and a local lady Rajita knew (an expert on this particular ritual) came to chant, and like the others was a doll. When they arrived, we went to lunch.

Jean and I picked a restaurant that had a patio by the little river in town. It was quite sunny that day and the big umbrellas were cranked open on the tables. After we ordered, the sun retreated and I lowered our umbrella. In the process of lowering it I looked up and saw a perfect round rainbow, just like a halo! There was no rain or rain clouds, just a perfectly round rainbow overhead. I have never seen this kind of rainbow in my life, until that day. Both Jean and I took this as a sign from God that Rajita was taking steps toward leaving her body.

After lunch we told everyone at the apartment about seeing the rainbow. Then we went upstairs and held Rajita's hand and told her. She smiled for the first time and astoundingly, looked beautiful. Previously her face had looked hard and stressed. Her face now was softening and there was radiance about her. So I took a bold chance at humor and told her she looked "marvelous."

I could tell she loved that and after some indecipherable mumblings she said, "You look marvelous, too." Then she nodded off. This was the only tender moment Jean and I experienced with her in that time and I know I will always cherish it. Her eyes were merely slits and we had to get close to her mouth to hear her talk, but we took this gift and treasured it as a golden bit of love.

## MAY 15: CONVERSATIONS ABOUT WATER

We are bone tired. Ulla greeted us at our usual eight o'clock meeting. She informed us that Rajita had drunk at least one gallon of water yesterday and through the night. Rajita's original intention was to not eat or drink until she passed so she would not drag on in pain and incapacitation, like both of our parents did. Some people live a long time—weeks—without food if they get lots of water.

Jean and I knew Rajita wanted us at her side to give her strength, love, and courage. Though she never used those words, we instinctively got the message loud and clear once we were there in person. I believed just our presence was helping her face her death. If she lingered, however, Jean and I would be heading back to our respective homes, Ulla would be gone on vacation, a stranger would be taking care of Rajita, and Rajita's money would be getting precariously low, since it was expensive to hire caregivers. That was not the scenario anyone wanted to happen.

Ulla, Jean, and I did not believe my sister was mentally tracking information clearly, and we knew Rajita was unaware of how much water she was drinking. When she did talk to the caregivers and the hospice nurse, Rajita could appear mentally sharp, especially if the people were not careful to read all her actions correctly.

Therefore, Jean and I decided to communicate to Rajita exactly how much water she was actually drinking each day. We broached this head-on with the truth. It was her choice whether she drank water or not, but we felt she needed to know exactly what she was doing. Jean and I also decided to tell her each day how many days were left before we needed to go home.

From the encounter with her the weeks before, we knew we had to deliver this news firmly. I did not have an attachment to what Rajita decided, but she was not following her original intention and we wanted her to know the effects on her quality of life if she should continue. What she decided to do with that information was her decision.

So with some fear and trepidation (and I must admit, deep sadness), Jean and I went to her bedroom. We each took her hand and got close to Rajita so she could hear us. We told her she was drinking about a gallon of water a day and if she continued, she could live many more weeks, but she would be without her friends who would need to leave eventually, and we would be gone, and so would Ulla. At first Rajita was not tracking and her eyes were barely open—only little slits. Then I decided to tell her she very well might run out of money. Well, with that statement her eyes flew open wide, and we were assaulted with the sight of her eyes being totally yellow, a result of her liver shutting down. I had never encountered anything that resembled eyes like those in my life, nor had Jean. It was truly frightening and ghastly to witness, especially with a loved one. It is one thing to intellectually understand about a dying person's organs shutting down and quite another to witness it first hand.

Rajita was agitated, but finally comprehended after about five minutes of our repeating the same information over and over that she was not following what was, in her religion, a solemn vow.

Jean and I called Ulla in to talk to her after that. Thank God again for Ulla! We left Rajita's bedroom shaken and drained. No words can give this moment the gravitas Jean and I experienced in delivering this information to Rajita. Our personal commitment was to be by her side and to help her cross in the manner she wanted. Jean and I were seriously trying to live up to this duty we volunteered to do, and to do it with grace, love, and care.

After a while Ulla came downstairs. She said Rajita asked her, "What is happening to my brain?" After that statement we knew we were right about Rajita not tracking mentally. From that moment on she took no more water, just a few ice chips and something to moisten her lips. Following that we had no more communication from Rajita whatsoever. She went inward faster and went into what hospice calls active dying.

## MAY 16: RAJITA COMMUNICATES THROUGH A DREAM

Ulla had the day off. Sherry came in during the day and would sleep over. We went up to Rajita's room and held her hand and once again sent her our love. Her face continued to soften in look and demeanor. She wasn't drinking water and was completely bedridden now. Previously she could use the portable toilet with the help of Ulla or Sherry. Now she was wearing Depends.

Every night I would go to sleep singing the HU and asking to be of service for Rajita. Singing the HU is a very powerful way to connect with Divine Love. I wanted Rajita to know I loved her. Hopefully she would feel my love (or Divine Love) through her dream state.

The night before our talk with her about the water, I dreamed about these many cats that peed copious amounts of urine on my carpet. I handled them in my dream with love and did not shame the little ones about this transgression. Then the dream faded with me peacefully cleaning up the urine. I remembered telling Jean I had a dream and I didn't know what it meant. My new cat family back in Atlanta was well behaved and used their litter pans faithfully. We had no occurrences of inappropriate peeing at our house.

I thought nothing more of the dream until we got to Rajita's apartment that day. Both Sherry and Ulla had noticed that for the amount of water Rajita had been drinking, she should have had more urine. (Caretakers and hospice monitor everything, including the amount of urine.) Since she could not use the portable toilet, Rajita had been holding her urine. We found this out when she asked for a catheter. With the catheter in place she finally released all the urine she was holding, and it was several pints.

This matched up with my dream. Cats are my symbol of love. Rajita was communicating to me through the dream state her embarrassment at urinating in her Depends. Ulla reminded Jean and me that throughout our lives we are taught not to pee in our pants. Now we were telling Rajita to do just that.

This dream also told me that even in her unconscious state Rajita was communicating with me. I needed to remember that; when her body died, communication could still take place. My beliefs are that as Soul there is no death and that love transcends different dimensions. One just needs the awareness of this and the ability to receive the love or messages the other Soul is trying to send.

That day Jean and I needed a longer time away from the watch of death. We took a long hike in the park after we saw Rajita that morning, we ate our lunch outside at a cute restaurant, and then we did something very normal— we went to a movie. After the movie we took another walk and headed back to Rajita's to say good night. She had been completely unresponsive since the day before. After we saw Rajita, Jean and I went back to our hotel and just collapsed.

## MAY 17: OUR LAST DAY IN ASHLAND

Sherry the night caretaker said that during the night Rajita said out loud, to no one in particular, "I am going to conk out today." No one really doubted her as she had orchestrated so much of her transition. It was our last day in Ashland. As usual, we told Rajita how many days were left before we were to go home. That day, we told her we were leaving tomorrow. Then we finished up the last minute details of things that had to be done before we left. Regardless of how long she lingered, everything would be taken care of for her and the disposition of her belongings.

That morning we asked one of the interns to drive us to the UPS store nearby that could ship big items. We needed to send one of Rajita's paintings to a dear friend of hers back East. This was around ten-thirty. At eleven we got a call from Ulla. Rajita's breathing had shifted and was shallower, indicating she could pass very soon. All of us piled back into the car and rushed back to her apartment. Hospice was called and the chanters stayed for the rest of the day.

The nurse arrived and examined Rajita. She confirmed Rajita could go in minutes or days. That morning, as Jean was in the bathroom getting ready for the day, I did my spiritual exercise of singing HU. I usually do not see things in my contemplations, but today I spontaneously saw myself helping Rajita out of her body. She was half in and half out. I was gently lifting her out of her body. Then the Soul Travel experience ended.

This was another confirmation for me that my mission was to help my sister make her transition. This whole week was just that, from clearing out her belongings, to quietly sending her love, to the incredibly difficult conversation about our leaving and her water intake. Our actions were part of a plan, helping Rajita to have courage, support, and love in her last days on Earth.

Jean and I said our last goodbyes to Rajita at eight that evening. We were leaving for the airport at seven the next morning. We told Sherry, the night caregiver, that we wanted to be called right away if Rajita died during the night. At the hotel we packed and showered, just in case we received the call of her passing. We didn't sleep. Both of us just tossed and turned and lay awake.

The call came at one in the morning, the ring sounding like a roar to our ears. Sherry told us our sister passed peacefully at quarter to one. Sherry had called the other people Rajita wanted at her side at death. Gayle volunteered to pick us up since it was the middle of the night. Sherry and Gayle bathed Rajita in the special oils she obtained weeks before from the monks in Hawaii. They also dressed her in the white sari Rajita had picked to be cremated in. Ulla had been called and so had the hospice nurse. In total there were nine women.

Rajita's bedroom was very small. The nine of us had just enough room to gather around her bed. The number of people was serendipitous, and the synchronistic events were still unfolding. All week long Ulla had lovingly cared for all the flowers Rajita received for her birthday. She cut away dead blooms and kept the dried flowers to use for a burial ceremony.

Rajita had gotten a dozen red roses on her birthday. Exactly nine roses were still left. Ulla suggested we do a loving ceremony right then to honor and send love to Rajita, and we all agreed. We each were given one of the red roses and one by one we took the petals and in loving, almost sacred silence, scattered them on my sister's body. The love in that room was palpable. Though all the women were of different religions and spiritual practices, each had a golden heart of love. And all their love was now flowing to the Soul that was Rajita.

After we scattered the rose petals, Ulla sang in German, "Let There Be Peace." Inwardly I sang the HU. Someone else did the Hindu chant, and we all said goodbye. At the very end of our intimate and precious ceremony the people from the funeral parlor came for Rajita's body. In accordance with her spiritual tradition her body had to be cremated within twenty-four hours of death.

We all talked for a few more minutes and then I tearfully said goodbye to the dear, strong women who had traveled to be there and helped us with this part of our journey with Rajita. Gayle drove us back to our hotel and said she would take us to the airport in the morning.

Jean and I got no sleep whatsoever. Around five-thirty in the morning Jean and I started calling back East to different family members and shared the news. I was also in charge of contacting all the people on Rajita's list to let them know she passed. While I was waiting for my flight at the airport, I made the calls on my mobile phone. What struck me most from those conversations was the fierce loyalty and respect Rajita commanded from people who knew her. All the people I called, including some she had not seen in twenty years, expressed the highest regards for her expertise in art and recalled how deeply she had affected their lives.

Rajita was loved and would be missed. Her mission in this lifetime seemed to be one of not only personal and spiritual growth, but also to be a catalyst for others to see the deeper meaning of life.

✳

EPILOGUE

J EAN AND I COULDN'T SLEEP ON THE PLANE COMING
home. By the time I got home and finally got to sleep
the next night I had been up for almost forty-eight hours.
When we touched down in Atlanta, Jean changed planes
for Syracuse. We hugged fiercely. Words could not express
the love, trauma, and grief we felt. Our five-year mission
was over. With tears in our eyes we went back to our respective families.

I had a car coming to pick me up, as I knew I'd be
shaken and have no energy for driving in Atlanta traffic.
I waited for my car at the curb, my eyes gritty from lack of
sleep and my body and mind just numb from all that happened. During that wait I was wondering how my sister
Rajita was doing in her new life. Was she okay? Was she
being taken care of?

At that very moment I saw a man step out of a van
with an Oregon license plate, throw a bunch of bags in
the back, get back in the van, and drive off. This was a
waking dream for me.

*Remember that waking dreams are God's way of communicating to you when you are awake. It is an occurrence that strikes a chord with you, giving you a message or teaching of some kind.*

I had never seen an Oregon license plate at the Atlanta airport before, and I saw this man and the van at the precise moment of my musings. The message came in loud and clear. Rajita was being taken care of and her "baggage" was being handled. To someone else this occurrence would hold no meaning. For me it meant the world.

My husband was waiting for me at the front door when I arrived home and greeted me with a bear hug. Unbeknownst to me, my good friends had hand delivered a beautiful Japanese maple tree and left it on my front step. It was their gift to me as a remembrance of my sister's life. I broke down and wept when I saw it and felt how much love and support I had experienced during this time.

Because I had decided not to emotionally run away from helping my sister cope with her illness and eventual death, I had received so many precious gifts of love and personal growth. My relationships with both Jean and Rajita got so much closer, and I deeply treasured that. I feel I grew spiritually, which is hard to articulate, but my fear of death diminished, and my ability to give from a very deep place at the core of my being grew to a new level. My perspective of what is important shifted, and I felt my capacity to love was growing. All this evolved for me from helping my sister Rajita.

We will all face the death of our body someday. The point of being on Earth is experience and growth. This is a hard school, but it can be a school of incredible growth for that very reason. I can only speak for myself, but I believe that by living with the conscious awareness that this life is a spiritual journey, I experience more love, more joy, and less fear. Most importantly, I realize my true self is Soul, not this body.

My experiences with spiritual Light, Sound, dreams, and Soul Travel that I have shared with you in this book have helped me throughout my entire life. These experiences have opened my heart to more love and wisdom. When God talks to you in any of these ways, it is for your growth. There is always a reason for the spiritual dance and communication. Know true communication from God is always for the good, the betterment of your life. Experiences that are from the Light and Sound of God will never nudge you to do something to hurt yourself or others.

Healthy boundaries are one example. They may seem (at the moment) hard to implement or hurtful, but if they keep you safe and protected from physical or emotional harm from others, they are for the good of the whole of life. You are part of the whole of life you need to love. Only you can communicate and follow through with your boundaries.

Life is a dance. What kind of dance do you want for your life? What kind of partner do you want on your journey here? The ego (which is based on mass conscious beliefs that may make you happy for a moment or a season) or connecting with the unchanging, deepest aspect of your journey here, Divine Love?

The dream I shared with you at the beginning of this book was right on every level. It inwardly prepared me for my incredibly hard mission and foretold I would emerge from this experience with new growth, which I am still experiencing.

Regardless of your religion or lack of one, let me leave you with these thoughts: No matter what is happening in your life now, you can choose to dance your life with God.

*You exist as Soul*
*because God loves you!*

*A Message from the Author,*
*Marian Massie*

# Please help me help the world!

🌿 **Tell** a friend about this book or buy it for your friend.

🌿 Go to **Amazon.com** and write a recommendation where the book is listed.

🌿 Write a positive comment about this book on your Facebook page, Twitter or any **social media** sites where you are a member. Tell them why you are recommending it and that they can buy it on Amazon.com or ask for it in any bookstore.

🌿 Email me a **testimonial** of your thoughts about this book to: *Marian@DancingWithGodTheBook.com*

🌿 **Write** Oprah, Ellen DeGeneres, or any other famous person you may know, including radio personalities, about this book. If you know them personally, please get me an introduction.

🌿 Email me the name of the **contact** person who can book me as a speaker for your church or organization.

If you found this book uplifting or beneficial in any way, please assist me in bringing more love, awareness and positive energy into this world. You can do this by helping me get *Dancing with God… A True Story* into more people's hands. I cannot do this alone! Action done by an individual, multiplied, creates enormous change. Your action is vital for this transformation of world consciousness to occur. Your simple step is the catalyst of creating change.

So here is what I suggest: choose to do as many of these action steps to get this book into the hands of as many people as you can.

I eagerly await your comments on this book and how it has positively impacted your life. Send your personal testimonials to:

Marian@DancingWithGodTheBook.com

Please note that by sending your email testimonials you are giving me permission to publish them in part or whole. Thank you from the bottom of my heart for helping me help others through your testimonials!

**www.marianmassie.com**

*Thank you in advance
for anything you can do to let the world
know about this book!*

## About the Author

**MARIAN MASSIE, CL.H.**
is the founder and CEO
of Advanced Perceptions, Inc.

A Clinical Hypnotherapist and Success Coach,
Marian has helped Fortune 500 executives,
entrepreneurs, lawyers, physicians, and individuals
all over the world achieve greater personal
and professional success since 1985.

Marian has authored another
groundbreaking book, *You Are Soul*.

She lives in Atlanta, Georgia,
with her husband Mark
and her two Ragdoll cats, Sam and Bailey.

**www.marianmassie.com**

CPSIA information can be obtained at www.ICGtesting.com
Printed in the USA
LVOW120720110113

315136LV00001B/15/P